Using
Qualitative Research
in Advertising

SECOND EDITION

For Mary Beth and Ken Morrison.
M. M.

To Ron Taylor, for 19 years of exceptional leadership,
mentorship, and friendship.
E. H.

To my family.
K. B. S.

To the students who have accompanied me on the journey for qualitative
understanding and have enriched my life by doing so.
R. T.

Using Qualitative Research in Advertising

Strategies, Techniques, and Applications

SECOND EDITION

Margaret A. Morrison
University of Tennessee, Knoxville

Eric Haley
University of Tennessee, Knoxville

Kim Bartel Sheehan
University of Oregon

Ronald E. Taylor
University of Tennessee, Knoxville

Los Angeles | London | New Delhi
Singapore | Washington DC

Los Angeles | London | New Delhi
Singapore | Washington DC

FOR INFORMATION:

SAGE Publications, Inc.
2455 Teller Road
Thousand Oaks, California 91320
E-mail: order@sagepub.com

SAGE Publications Ltd.
1 Oliver's Yard
55 City Road
London, EC1Y 1SP
United Kingdom

SAGE Publications India Pvt. Ltd.
B 1/I 1 Mohan Cooperative Industrial Area
Mathura Road, New Delhi 110 044
India

SAGE Publications Asia-Pacific Pte. Ltd.
33 Pekin Street #02-01
Far East Square
Singapore 048763

Acquisitions Editor: Matthew Byrnie
Associate Editor: Nathan Davidson
Production Editor: Brittany Bauhaus
Copy Editor: Megan Granger
Typesetter: Hurix Systems Pvt. Ltd.
Proofreader: Sandy Zilka
Cover Designer: Bryan Fishman
Marketing Manager: Liz Thornton
Permissions Editor: Karen Ehrmann

Printed in the United States of America

*Library of Congress Cataloging-in-Publication
Data*

Using qualitative research in advertising :
strategies, techniques, and applications/
Margaret A. Morrison ... [et al.].—2nd ed.

p. cm.
Includes bibliographical references and index.

ISBN 978-1-4129-8724-0 (pbk. : alk. paper)

1. Advertising—Research. 2. Market research—
Methodology. 3. Qualitative research.
I. Morrison, Margaret A.

HF5814.U78 2012

659.1072—dc23

2011024469

This book is printed on acid-free paper.

11 12 13 14 15 10 9 8 7 6 5 4 3 2 1

Contents

Preface   ix
Acknowledgments   xv

1. **Introduction and Overview**   1
   A Brief History of Account Planning   4
   The Function of Planning   7
   The Role of Research in the Day-to-Day Activities
       of Account Planners   8
   Stages of Account Planning   10
   Examples   12
   Account Planning as Part of the Overall
       Marketing Effort   17
   Organization of This Book   18

2. **A Qualitative View of the World**   23
   Theory and Data Analysis   23
   Inside the Qualitative World   24
   Assumptions That Bind   25
   Qualitative Words   27
   The Qualitative Approach   28
   Qualitative Methods   29
   Qualitative Data   30
   Analysis of Qualitative Data   30
   Multiple Versus Mixed Methods   36
   Summary   38
   Key Terms   39
   Exercises   40
   Related Reading   41

3. **Ethnographic Methods for Advertising Research**   43
   Getting Emic   43
   Participant Observation   45
   General Issues With Participant Observation Studies   47

Panel Studies		56
General Issues With Panel Studies		58
Getting Ready to Listen		60
Summary		61
Key Terms		61
Exercises		63
Related Reading		64
4.	**Listening to Consumers**	**65**
	The Qualitative Interview	65
	Characteristics of Qualitative Interviewing	66
	Getting Ready to Interview	68
	Conducting the Interview	71
	Introducing Objects	74
	Ending the Interview	75
	Analyzing the Transcripts	75
	Interviewing Groups	80
	When You Can't Gain Access to the Natural Setting	83
	Clarifying the Social Role of Qualitative Interviewer	84
	Summary	85
	Key Terms	86
	Exercises	86
	Related Reading	88
5.	**Projective and Elicitation Techniques**	**89**
	History of Projective Techniques	92
	Types of Projective Techniques	94
	Advantages and Disadvantages of Projective Techniques	107
	Data Analysis	109
	Summary	113
	Key Terms	113
	Exercises	115
	Related Reading	116
6.	**Qualitative Research Online**	**117**
	Focus Groups and Interviews	117
	Online Focus Groups	119
	Planning the Group and the Role of the Moderator	124

Asynchronous Groups 126
Depth Interviewing 132
Summary 140
Key Terms 140
Exercises 141
Related Reading 142

7. **Using Research to Inspire Great Creative Work** **143**
Writing and Presenting the Creative Brief 143
The Role of the Account Planner 144
The Role of the Creative Brief 145
The Basics of the Creative Brief 149
The Language of the Creative Brief 154
Assessing the Creative Brief 156
Presenting the Brief 158
Enhancing the Creative Brief 160
Finding the Most Compelling Way to Deliver
 the Strategy 160
A Final Check 162
Summary 162
Key Terms 163
Exercises 164
Related Reading 164

8. **Balancing Ideals and Real-World Constraints** **165**
Budget 165
Redundancy and Budget Constraints 166
Over-Recruiting 168
Cost-Effective Research Based on Client Rosters 169
Scheduling 170
Using Multiple Researchers to Save Time 170
Getting Permission to Ask the Questions You Need
 and Avoiding Questions You Don't 172
Summary 176
Key Terms 176
Exercises 177
Related Reading 178

9. Evaluating the Work of Planners and
     Parting Thoughts   179
   How It Is and How It Should Be   180
   Evaluation Measures Used in Award-Winning Planning   181
   Parting Thoughts   183
   Thoughts on Building Your Toolbox   185

   Appendix 1: Conducting a Long Interview   187

   Appendix 2: Putting Your Skills to Use   197

   **Appendix 3: Disney's Animal Kingdom
      Theme Park: A Case Study**   201

   References   207

   Index   213

   About the Authors   217

Preface

OUR STORY

For all of us, our interest in qualitative research extends back at least to our doctoral studies. And, given that we're all full professors now, that adds up to more than 75 years of observing, interviewing, and interacting with people who are on the receiving end of persuasive messages, all in the hope of understanding what moves them.

Not surprisingly, our interests find their way into the classroom and drive the topics we research. It's pretty standard today to find a research class in most advertising curricula. But at the time we wrote the first edition of this book, those classes tended to be quantitative in nature, largely with a focus on survey research and analysis of secondary quantitative sources. While qualitative research was considered, it was usually contained to a unit or two that gave instruction on how to conduct focus groups. The ideas that drive qualitative research were seldom explored in depth, and proper techniques for conducting the type of research we do were lacking. It was a situation that perplexed us as we were positive that understanding consumers was key to creating successful campaigns, and qualitative research was central to such an understanding. When we looked at research methods texts at that time that were aimed at students and professionals, they often included a cursory discussion about the merits of qualitative methods, but lacked real direction into how you did it or why it was a perfect fit for figuring out the idiosyncrasies of human beings.

Coinciding with our unease was the emergence of account planning in the United States, which was just starting to take off back in the 1990s. Account planners try to understand people, a goal we shared with them. It's no wonder, then, that we all gravitated toward account planning. To us, it represented a way to combine the things we loved—advertising and qualitative research. We attended a professional meeting of planners where one of the major themes was the dearth of employees trained in ways to identify and develop consumer insights for strategic purposes. Seeing the needs of the industry, coupled with those we had noted among our students, led to a decision to write a book. A book that shared our vision regarding qualitative research, one that told people how to do it and do it well. A book that would help students interested in planning as well as planners who wanted to be better at their jobs. That was the story behind the first edition.

When we first became interested in account planning it was still mainly contained to full-service agencies in larger metropolitan areas. That advertising centric focus was evident in the first edition. But the environment in which planners operate has changed, expanding into areas such as product packaging, sales promotions, and a plethora of alternative media. In short, it's become more of a branding environment as opposed to one limited to advertising. Brand identity develops via a network of meaning systems; we've tried to reflect this new perspective in the second edition.

NEW IN THE SECOND EDITION

In addition to expanding the focus of the book from advertising to branding, many new things are noteworthy in this edition.

- Throughout the book, references have been updated to reflect current views of qualitative research in the marketing environment. The examples we added include products, services, and experiences; they were selected to illustrate that the utility of planning extends far beyond advertising.
- Practitioners and students sometimes confuse using a qualitative "method" with a qualitative approach to conducting research. We contend that there is a difference between mixed methods and multiple methods, and we attempt to clarify this distinction in a new section of Chapter 2.
- Recruitment of participants for qualitative research can be akin to navigating a minefield. In this addition, we've paid more attention to the selection of participants and

their recruitment for interviews, ethnographies, and online research. We've also included a section in Chapter 8 that addresses the recruitment of "easy" versus the "right" participants.

- Unlike procedures for quantitative research where a researcher is expected to remain objective in the research process, we believe the role of the researcher in qualitative research should be acknowledged and embraced. In keeping with this a discussion of the social role of a qualitative researcher has been added in Chapter 4.

- Because of the numerous ethical issues involved in conducting any research—particularly for some qualitative methods—we've expanded this edition to include more ethics-related examples and added new exercises specifically devoted to this topic.

- Due to the changes in conducting online research, Chapter 6, which deals with conducting interviews and focus groups online, has been completely rewritten. The new version recognizes technological changes as well as newer forms of social media that weren't in existence when we wrote the first edition.

- Our chapter on projective techniques has also been expanded to consider how these approaches can be used with new media and how other elicitation techniques might be useful in identifying consumer insights.

- A oversight in the first edition was that there was no discussion on how to evaluate qualitative research and the work of planners. We've rectified that in the second edition in Chapter 9. In it we rely on work we've conducted on how planners' work is and should be evaluated. We also rely on an analysis of award-winning account planning cases to see what metrics they employed to gage the effectiveness of planning.

FOR INSTRUCTORS AND PROFESSIONALS

We've always been of the mindset that the best way to understand a research method it to get your hands dirty. In other words, practice using it. With that in mind, we've updated the exercises at the end of each chapter in this second edition to give individuals that opportunity. Feedback from our first edition indicated that readers wanted to know more about the nuts and bolts of qualitative research. So, we added three appendices to give life to techniques described in the text.

Analyzing qualitative data was something that readers wanted to know more about. So, to accompany the Chapter 4 discussion of interviewing, Appendix 1 contains an assignment appropriate for either students or entry-level planners, an example of an interview that might stem from such an assignment, an annotated interview transcript with notes critiquing the interview, and a sample summary write-up of an interview with accompanying documentation. Essentially, it's a comprehensive exercise that can be used at several points where readers come in contact with qualitative research. For those conducting primary research, it allows one to apply techniques learned in this text from research design to analysis. For others who are conducting secondary analysis (in this case relying on transcripts generated by another researcher), it offers insight into evaluating an existing text. In all cases it offers tips for critiquing an interview, how to make your own interviews better, and how to analyze the multitude of pages that often result from a qualitative interview.

Appendix 2, "Putting Your Skills to Use," includes three assignments that are longer than those found at the end of individual chapters. In term of focus, the assignments are varied. The first one deals with a once popular product (wrist watches) that is no longer seen as vital among a younger target market. Those considering the assignment are asked to identify a target market, set objectives for research, and develop a research plan that will lead to insights that could reinvigorate the product. The second assignment asks individuals to determine the meaning of dogs to the people who own them in order to decide whether a large consumer beverage company should enter the pet industry with a fortified drinking water designed especially for dogs. The final assignment is for a prominent spice company. This company wants to grow its business, but in order to do so, it must figure out how to induce younger adults to begin cooking at home. All three of these assignments call for a different application of qualitative research techniques and enable readers to see how qualitative research is applicable for a number of marketing problems.

Finally, Appendix 3 presents a case study that has used qualitative research to solve a problem. In this case, it's how to get adults who visit Walt Disney World in Florida to extend their stay to include a day at Disney's Animal Kingdom Theme Park. Readers are taken step by step through the problem, the objectives that stem from it, and the research plan that was devised to solve the problem. As opposed to talking in generalities about the research plan as many texts do, this example discusses in detail how research resulted in an insight that led to a creative strategy, which is exactly what planners do.

We hope you like the second edition of this book. We liked the first one, but think that the changes we've made to this version have resulted in a better way to tell you how to do what you want to do.

Good luck,
—Margie, Eric, Kim, and Ron

Acknowledgments

We acknowledge the assistance of SAGE Publications professionals Matthew Byrnie, Nathan Davidson, Liz Thornton, Bryan Fishman, Karen Ehrmann, and Brittany Bauhaus, the many account planners and creative teams who have shared their stories with us, and our students, as we updated the first edition of the book.

The authors and SAGE would also like to acknowledge the contributions of the following reviewers:

Danielle Sarver Coombs, *Kent State University*

Jennifer Lovrinic, *Temple University*

Julie O'Neil, *Texas Christian University*

Brian Charles Tringali, *The George Washington University*

1

Introduction and Overview

Advertising, as you've probably noticed, surrounds every facet of your life. Indeed, industry estimates suggest that global advertising expenditures will exceed $500 billion in 2011, with more than a quarter of that in the United States alone ("GroupM Forecasts," 2010). That translates into millions of ads, all vying for the attention of consumers. In some instances, advertisers are looking for the attention of specific, targeted groups of consumers (e.g., adults aged 25–54 who are liberal, recycle regularly, entertain at least twice a month, and have minimum household incomes of $75,000). In other instances, targeted audiences may be more general (e.g., working moms). Regardless of the target, marketers have become savvy in using research to create messages that are relevant, timely, and motivating to the audience they want to reach.

And advertising hasn't just grown; the whole concept of what it's good for is changing. Today's emphasis on "branding" has served to heighten the value of advertising. A strong brand is much more than a name that identifies a product. A brand is a concept that exists only in a consumer's mind and is separate from the physical product or company with which it is associated. That concept is made up of a whole web of meanings that are associated with a particular product, company, or service provider and develop over time. Marketers invest in advertising and other forms of marketing communication to build strong brands. The benefits of a strong brand to a marketer can be consumer loyalty, marketing efficiency, longevity, and profitability.

Think about brands that you, as a consumer, really like. Chances are they have meaning to you in several ways. Maybe they are brands you can count on, brands that make you feel good, brands that remind you of home, brands that make you feel special, or myriad other personal meanings. In some positive way, these brands are relevant to you. Marketing professionals have found that strong, valuable brands have such aforementioned dimensions. For example, Y&R, a major multinational advertising agency, has mapped brands along such dimensions for 20 years using its proprietary tool, the Brand Asset Valuator. Strong brands in the Brand Asset Valuator are those that consumers know well, that consumers feel are particularly relevant to their lives, and that have strong positive affective dimensions (i.e., positive feelings).

This is a book about how to use a particular type of research—qualitative research—to inspire great advertising and build strong brands. Qualitative research refers to "the meanings, concepts, definitions, characteristics, metaphors, symbols, and descriptions of things" (Berg, 1989, p. 2). It is an approach to research that uses a variety of methods and involves an interpretive, naturalistic approach to whatever is the focus of study (Denzin & Lincoln, 1994). Its greatest utility is in discovering underlying meanings and patterns in relationships. The character of qualitative research makes it and its associated methods extremely useful for uncovering complex consumer insights that can lead to successful branding.

We think that qualitative research is the best way to understand how a brand is or isn't relevant to a consumer, how consumers truly feel about brands, and how brands are relevant to the way they live their lives. Concepts such as "relevance" are meaning-based ideas, and meaning is constructed by humans. Take, for example, the letter T. To most people, it's an important letter in that constructing a sentence without it would be difficult. (That sentence alone contains 16 Ts.) But all the authors of this book have some association with the University of Tennessee, and for us, a T has some additional meanings: the color orange (the university's signature color), the power T (which is always capitalized), the Volunteers (the name associated with most of the university's athletic programs), technology (the university's e-mail program is called "tmail") . . . and a lot of other stuff. If you're a marketer trying to sell something in Tennessee, you really need to be aware of the meaning of a *T*. And if you wanted to sell something in Texas, *T* would take on whole new meanings (e.g., longhorn cattle, *Friday Night Lights*, etc.). We truly feel that there's no better way to understand the *T*s of the world than through qualitative research. That's what makes this book important.

In writing this book, we've tried to adopt a consumer perspective, because it's hard to build a brand without consumers. And we're convinced that great advertising comes only from an understanding of consumers' wants and needs. In order to understand those wants and needs, the consumer needs to be consulted and integrated at virtually every step of the research process. In short, the strategies and techniques outlined in this book are based on something called an account planning philosophy. Central to this concept is the idea that in order to understand consumers, you need to understand how they make and interpret meaning and how those meanings are transferred to brands through things such as advertising. We'll talk about this philosophy in just a moment.

We wrote this book for several different audiences. Primarily, account planners will find this book a valuable resource, particularly given the few formal training programs that are offered today. In a national U.S. survey of account planners that we conducted, only 45% of respondents reported that they had received formal on-the-job training (55% didn't receive any formal training), and 95% reported receiving only informal on-the-job training. Fewer than half of respondents reported receiving training in qualitative research methods. The area of qualitative methods was one of the most cited when we asked planners, "In what areas do you feel you need more training?" Yet our survey also uncovered that qualitative methods are commonly used by account planners. Given that account planners are often involved in qualitative research but receive little training in how to use qualitative methods, we saw the need for a book that planners can turn to as they go about the difficult task of trying to develop consumer insights.

Of course, account planners aren't the only ones who might find value in this book. Others who might find this book helpful include research suppliers who, given their relationship with account planners, want to understand the role of qualitative research a bit better; advertising agencies, who will find it a useful addition to their reference libraries; and training programs and universities offering classes in advertising.

A BRIEF HISTORY OF ACCOUNT PLANNING

In order to put our later discussions of particular types of research into context, a brief overview of the history and nature of account planning is in order. Account planning was developed in the mid-1960s and can be traced to the U.K. offices of two advertising agencies— J. Walter Thompson and Boase Massimi Pollitt (now BMP DDB; Steel, 1998). Account planning originated from a need to better understand the increasingly complex consumer landscape, synergize research, and bring a consumer focus into the process of message generation.

By the 1960s, society was undergoing great changes, and that meant that the nature of consumerism was also changing. Think about it: Before World War II, women stayed home and cared for their kids, and men headed off to earn the household paycheck. That all changed with World War II. More and more women entered the workplace, and the dynamics of the household—especially with regard to product purchasing—changed dramatically. Instead of cooking meals from scratch and keeping a spotless home, modern working women looked for foods that required little preparation and products that helped cut down on the time it took to clean house. As a result, whole new product categories emerged that catered to the needs of these women. Then the women's liberation movement changed the landscape even more. Suddenly, advertisers weren't sure how to speak to modern women.

That's just one example; we don't want to give you the idea that account planning grew solely out of the women's liberation movement. Other cultural changes, such as the leveling of racial attitudes, the growth of technology, the emergence of the credit industry, and the rise of health and fitness concerns, were also occurring. The fact is that the entire social landscape was changing, and the influence on advertising and consumer purchasing habits was dramatic. That's even truer today, and evidence abounds showing that consumers don't adopt just one lifestyle or consume products according to a single set of attitudes (Piirto, 1990).

The business landscape of the 1960s was also changing. Parity was becoming evident in many product categories. For example, if you walked down the canned vegetable aisle in a grocery store, you might see three different options for green beans when before there had been only one. As product categories approached parity, the need arose to educate consumers about differences between brands that transcended the product's physical characteristics.

The role of market research also evolved, although not necessarily in a good way. Consumer research was being somewhat diluted across the marketing, advertising, and media research departments of both advertising agencies and clients. The number of independent companies conducting market research (i.e., research suppliers) escalated. These companies specialized in generating and selling information about consumers. One of the biggest purchasers of this information was advertising agencies. As a result, advertising agencies found themselves deluged with information, both from their internal research departments and from new, external agencies. Although this information was useful to ad agencies for learning more about consumers, the surge in available research resulted in agencies being so inundated with data that the account management team—which was in charge of coordinating the agency's efforts—was often not using data in the most efficient manner.

The account team wasn't the only one having trouble processing and using all that research. Lisa Fortini-Campbell (2001) notes that members of creative departments grew resistant to research that they saw as impeding their art. In part, this resistance stemmed from the way research was being used, not from the volume of it. Research was being used to copy test advertisements rather than to develop advertising. So research was being used to correct or shoot down ads that creatives already had invested a substantial amount of time in instead of being used in a diagnostic manner. And when research was used in the early stages of advertising development, it often went no further than the token focus group. Creatives often viewed the research imposed on them—whether from internal or external research factions—as lacking a basic understanding of the consumer and the problem at hand. The deluge of research information, coupled with the misuse of research in the creative process, meant that agencies were continuing to produce advertising without fully understanding what drove these new, complex consumers and what they needed in a changing marketplace.

Account planning, then, grew out of the changing consumer and business environments, coupled with the advertising agency's need for a single department to assemble and analyze relevant product data holistically and apply it to the day-to-day decision making on an account. In addition, account planning's popularity is attributable to the fact that the presence of an account planning department positions agencies as having exceptional creative solutions and sets them apart from competitors during the all-important stage of pitching new business (Barry, Peterson, & Todd, 1987; Maxwell, Wanta, & Bentley, 2000). Agencies with account planning departments essentially integrate functions formerly conducted by other departments in the agency or by outside market research consultants and seek to add a consumer perspective to all aspects of advertising development. This integration allows agencies to position themselves as strategic partners with their clients and to retain control over business that might otherwise be contracted out to independent research companies.

And so, account planning developed, gained in popularity, and spread to the rest of Europe during the 1970s. In 1982, account planning was "discovered" by Jay Chiat of Chiat/Day and introduced to the United States, where it was widely embraced (Steel, 1998). According to the Account Planning Group U.S. (the APG-US was the original professional association of account planners), by 1995, more than 250 people were employed in account planning in the United States, a figure that grew to more than 1,000 in 1999. While no recent numbers exist as to the current size of the discipline, account planning departments are now fairly common in the U.S. advertising industry. A recent survey of planners identified full-service agencies, creative boutiques, digital and multicultural agencies, and the client side all as places where planners work (LeFevre, Lee, Averell, & Toth, 2010). And planners aren't located only in large cities: Virtually every medium-sized agency and many small ones employ account planners (Nelson & Kent, 1999).

While planning "grew" out of advertising, today, it is used to understand all aspects of a client's business, such as corporate culture, management's values, the meaning of products to the workers who make them, and other important information that can inform message strategy development. Oftentimes, as a discipline becomes established, traditional job titles are replaced with catchy ones that differentiate one company from another. As a testament that planning has come of age, the title of account planner has evolved; brand strategist, strategic planner, brand planner, and (our favorite) brand anthropologist are all titles an account planner may hold. For simplicity's sake, we're going to refer to these folks throughout this book as account planners.

THE FUNCTION OF PLANNING

What exactly do account planners do? Account planners function as liaisons between the account executive and the creative department, and between the creative department and the consumer. Account planners are both researchers and strategists. In theory, account planners are fully integrated members of the account and creative teams. In practice, the structure of planning across agencies varies somewhat: In some agencies, the planning function leans more toward account management, and in others, planners are considered members of creative departments (Kover & Goldberg, 1995). Nevertheless, it is generally agreed that a planner is a point person in the process of developing message strategy, the

> primary contact with the outside world; the person who, through personal background, knowledge of all pertinent information, and overall experience, is able to bring a strong consumer focus to all advertising decisions. (White, 1995, p. 18)

The primary responsibility of planners is to understand the target audience and then represent it throughout the entire campaign development process. In fact, account planners work so closely with the target audiences they study that they are often referred to as "consumer advocates" (Kover, James, & Sonner, 1997). This intensive interaction with consumers and creative strategy development distinguishes account planners from more traditional market researchers (Barry et al., 1987; Capon & Scammon, 1979).

In fact, in addition to the other titles we identified, account planners are also known as creative researchers or strategic researchers.

Account planners attempt to understand and represent the target audience through the use of market and research data in areas such as the product, the category, the market, the competition, and the client. The understanding that flows from the research that account planners conduct leads to usable insights that can help creative and account management teams produce communication campaigns that are relevant to the target market. Effective consumer insights elicit reactions that motivate consumers to try to continue buying a product.

THE ROLE OF RESEARCH IN THE DAY-TO-DAY ACTIVITIES OF ACCOUNT PLANNERS

Account planners use a variety of research techniques to identify and understand consumer insights. In this capacity, they rely heavily on qualitative research, which provides the opportunity for intimate consumer contact in a less structured environment and allows for insight into the more emotional aspects of a brand. These techniques include traditional approaches, such as one-on-one interviewing and focus groups, as well as more innovative approaches, such as accompanied shopping, word associations, use of facilitation devices, video montages, projective techniques, and consumer diaries. The use of experts (e.g., key informants, semioticians, ethnographers, and cultural anthropologists) is also common; although these people might not work in market research, they often offer unique insights into a particular consumer situation. Account planners also track data from long-term studies on social and cultural changes that may be linked to advertising success. They are skilled at identifying and keeping abreast of trends related to a client's business. While doing their jobs, they conduct primary research and utilize secondary research sources such as published market reports, usage and attitude surveys, and awareness tracking studies.

The variety of research techniques used by account planners suggests two things. First, no single research technique can do everything; recognizing the advantages and disadvantages of each method is important. All sources of information are valuable, but they are also flawed because they are limited in scope and seldom yield the total answer to a given problem. Knowledge of the various research approaches is necessary to understand the scope of a consumer's personal experience and neutralize biases ("Healthy Research," 1982). Although we know that planners rely primarily on interviews and focus groups, smart planners know these approaches won't always yield the information they are trying to uncover. In fact, a few years back, at the annual convention of a planning association, several of the topics discussed dealt with the overuse of focus groups, the gist of the idea being that planners were using these groups without really considering whether they were the best way to tap into consumer insights.

Second, planners must be familiar with alternative research methods so they can intelligently evaluate the array of research options available to them. It is important to remember that qualitative research is not synonymous with just focus groups. Innovation, in the life of a planner, means finding the best and most appropriate way of talking to consumers, one that will yield the information that will lead to a great creative strategy. Often, that means much more than conducting focus groups or interviews. The number of new research techniques on the market is startling, and planners must be able to make cogent choices among varying options as they go about the important business of uncovering consumer insights. We hope this book will help you make these choices.

Although many of the techniques used by account planners are similar to those used by other research functions in an agency, account planning differs from more traditional research in that the research incorporated becomes part of the process instead of being used in an advisory or evaluative capacity. In this way, the account planner brings consumers into the process of creating a campaign and gives them a voice (hence the "consumer advocate" label planners sometimes have). For example, though more traditional research can produce consumer insights, an account planner takes these consumer insights, interprets them, and advises the creative team about how they can be used to develop creative strategy. In essence, the research used by account planners is more focused and integral to problem solving than is the case with traditional research, and the ability of planners to contribute intelligent

insights to their findings determines whether they are full partners in the creative process. As part of a team that works closely
together, planners often find they are aided in their interpretations of data by input from account managers, creatives, clients, or
agency management.

Although this book focuses on using qualitative research in
an innovative manner to develop creative strategies, you need
to know that innovation doesn't end with simply being research
savvy. Innovation also means being alert and aware of your
research surroundings so that you can make connections between
seemingly unconnected things. These are the types of connections
that help you uncover the consumer insights that lead to great
advertising.

STAGES OF ACCOUNT PLANNING

Account planning is aimed at generating consumer insights during two key phases of the campaign process: brand/creative strategy development and evaluation of campaign effectiveness. Lisa
Fortini-Campbell (2001), in her book about generating consumer
insights, *Hitting the Sweet Spot*, further divides the brand/creative
strategy development stage into the following stages: (a) discover-
ing/defining the advertising task, (b) preparing the creative brief,
(c) developing the creative, and (d) presenting the advertising to
the client. The techniques discussed in other chapters of this book
have differing degrees of utility depending on the stage of account
planning. In advance of these chapters, it is important to differentiate what happens at each stage.

Brand/strategy development is the main aspect of a planner's
job because it lays the groundwork for creative executions that
effectively communicate to consumers in a way that is relevant
and meaningful. Fortini-Campbell (2001) notes that a planner
must first gather and assimilate information about consumers and
their environment from every source available. She mentions the
importance of reviewing such things as secondary research and
sales data and of conducting primary research to find out everything possible about the environment the product inhabits. Pam
Scott (1999), a leader in the field of account planning, notes that

the target market's relationship with the product, the brand, the product category, and any cultural influences must all be considered prior to determining creative strategy. Research at this point is imperative in order to discover what communication needs to occur with consumers: One must know the problem before one can diagnose and treat it.

After research has been conducted, a planner must assemble, organize, and interpret it in such a way that consumer insights are highlighted and extraneous information not important to developing strategy is culled. To streamline this process, the planner prepares a creative brief. The purpose of the brief is to help guide the creative team as it conceptualizes advertising strategy designed to meet the objectives of the campaign. Scott (1999) notes that possible components of a creative brief focus on answers to the following questions: Why is the product being advertised? What is the advertising supposed to do? Who is the target market? What is known about the target market that will help with the advertising? What is the main thought that needs to be expressed? What are possible ways to communicate the main thought in the advertising?

It is also important to note that the creative brief is more than just the answers to these questions. According to Steel (1998), a brief is an ad to influence the creative team. Along this line, Scott (1999) notes that the brief should tell a story about the product's target audience but that a planner must keep in mind that the real target audience for the creative brief is the people who will read and use it, namely, the creative team. She recommends the use of humor, stories, and anecdotes designed to inspire the creative team and delivered in an innovative manner.

Once the brief has been delivered to the creative team, rough versions of the advertisements can be prepared. But the planner's job does not end with simply delivering the brief. As advertisements are developed, the planner's function at this stage is to verify with the target market that ads and other communication tactics are relevant and effective. All good advertising and communications campaigns begin with clearly set objectives; to be considered successful, the campaign must meet these objectives. While consumers are fickle and no advertising is a sure bet, practitioners and clients want as much of a guarantee as is possible to ensure that the message strategy of a campaign is on target.

Hence, the planner tests rough versions of ads against the target market. In evaluating the creative with the target, a planner might conduct group or one-on-one interviews with consumers in order to check that the advertisements are actually articulating the message strategy and are on track to reach the goals of the campaign. During these interviews, rough or "comp" versions of the ads are shown to participants, followed by intensive questioning on the part of the planner. It's worth noting that although this discussion of evaluation has focused on evaluating the creative in rough or comp forms, planners also evaluate the consumer's response to the campaign during and after its run. According to Douglas Atkin (1997), a noted figure in the field of account planning, "planners' ultimate responsibility is accountability for effectiveness" (p. 34).

Account planners are also often involved in presenting advertisements to potential or existing clients. Fortini-Campbell (2001) notes that at this stage, the planner represents the consumer's point of view and helps explain how the advertisements under consideration are in line with the campaign strategy. Planners also offer the client insights concerning how the campaign will perform with the target audience once it has been executed. It's worth mentioning here that the presence of an account planner at a business pitch for a new account often results in the agency winning the account.

EXAMPLES

To get an idea of the importance of conducting research prior to developing brand/creative strategy, one needs only to look at some case histories of clients who have benefited from the insights uncovered by planning. In recent years, awards specifically aimed at recognizing the role of account planning have been established. In the United States, these awards started with the Account Planning Group (i.e., APG-US). This organization was subsumed by the American Association of Advertising Agencies (4A's), which oversees an annual competition expressly for account planners. Awards are given on the basis of insight, creativity, and effectiveness. In selecting finalists for the awards, judges consider the business background of the product or service for which the campaign was designed, the communication objectives of the campaign, descriptions of brand and consumer insights that have been developed, and explanations of the creative strategy and guidelines for campaign evaluation. Several high-profile campaigns have earned the attention of the APG-US based on the contribution of account planning to the final marketing solution.

MoneyGram

If you've ever sent someone money electronically, you know that your options are limited to a couple of companies that do business in this category. The best known of these is Western Union, which in the 1990s enjoyed an 80% market share and outspent its major competitor, MoneyGram, three to one on advertising. Western Union also had twice as many locations as MoneyGram and an incredible 99% awareness level among consumers (compared with MoneyGram's 60% awareness; "Campbell Mithun Esty: MoneyGram," 1999).

Even though MoneyGram's sales had been declining for more than 2 years, it did have one advantage over Western Union: MoneyGram's service was cheaper than comparable service from Western Union. And MoneyGram's price included a free phone card and 10-word message to the recipient of the money transfer. However, while price was important to the target audience for the brand, on the surface, it didn't lend itself well to forming the basis of the brand's image.

The advertising agency Campbell Mithun Esty (CME) faced the challenge of transforming MoneyGram's price advantage from a product feature into a brand image. Planners from the agency went to urban neighborhoods to talk to MoneyGram's primary target market: African American women. Taking an ethnographic approach, they sought to understand these women's lives and to gain insight into their experiences with electronic money transfers and their feelings about Western Union and MoneyGram.

Several key findings emerged from their research. First, these women felt taken advantage of. This was true of their general feeling toward life as well as their wire transfer experiences. These women took care of those around them, but they sometimes couldn't help but feel a bit resentful about it. In helping their family and friends by wiring money, they were, in essence, giving away their hard-earned cash. And they had to pay a fee to do so! So it's no wonder that the women saw themselves as "givers" and wire transfers as "takers." This was particularly the view they held of Western Union, the category dominator. The same sentiments were voiced over and over by the target market.

It was the insight that the target market felt taken advantage of that formed the basis for the subsequent advertising that CME developed. The basis of the strategy was to make MoneyGram's cost advantage synonymous with giving back to these women. This was a strategy that worked on both rational (i.e., the cost savings) and emotional (i.e., giving as opposed to taking) levels. The executions featured a grandmotherly character who gave advice and looked out for the women in the target. This approach was supplemented by a donation program for a group with which the target market was familiar: the Boys & Girls Clubs of America. Both qualitative and quantitative measures were used to track the success of the campaign, which resulted in a sales growth for MoneyGram after only 2 months.

De Beers Group Marketing

Account planning is also good at identifying cultural idiosyncrasies that can jeopardize a client's chance at success. Such was the case for JWT Mumbai, whose client De Beers Group Marketing wanted to break into the Indian market for weddings ("JWT Mumbai," 2008). De Beers is primarily known as a company that sells diamonds, and while it was the No. 1 diamond company in the United States, it faced several obstacles in India. The first was that India is a conservative country where personal choice takes a back seat to tradition. Second, Indian tradition calls for gold—not diamonds—as the adornment of choice for a bride. This had been the case for centuries. The challenge for JWT Mumbai was to change this mind-set and create a preference for diamond jewelry.

To better understand the market, JWT commissioned a usage and attitude survey. Going into the project, the agency was under the assumption that parents were the decision makers when it came to weddings, since they traditionally foot the bill. But the survey revealed that the bride herself had as much say about wedding jewelry as her mother. Other trends supported this finding; engagements were becoming longer, brides were taking a more active role in planning their weddings, and females engaged to be married were becoming much more comfortable with their future in-laws. And, most importantly, brides viewed diamonds as contemporary and stylish.

JWT planners next used qualitative research, namely, focus groups and elicitation devices, to determine whether the trend data was accurate. They verified that brides who wore a lot of gold jewelry were perceived as traditional, obedient, and meek. The bride who wore traditional attire (gold) was seen as doing the right thing and not necessarily having the wedding she wanted. "Diamond Brides," however, were seen as elegant, extroverted, and confident. Diamonds signified high status, a sense of personal style, and an aspect of casual informality that didn't carry the stressful baggage of tradition. Planners determined that most Indian brides weren't happy on their wedding days (too much stress from having to keep up with traditional expectations), but diamonds represented a way for a bride to have a voice and enjoy her special day. This was attractive to younger Indian females.

As a result of its research, the JWT team developed the concept of the "Diamond Bride." These were happy brides who rejoiced in their weddings while maintaining some measure of personal independence. The creative idea presented diamonds as the stone for brides who had spark. The ads themselves delivered on this idea, showing brides who reveled in their big days, wearing diamonds and bestowing kisses on their new husbands (kissing between newly married couples was not a tradition in Indian culture). The product figured prominently in the celebration and, as such, was legitimized by the advertising. The creative was executed through short films, TV infomercials, advertorials in magazines, and public relations. In a particularly innovative tactic, India's three top fashion designers provided their own interpretations of the Diamond Bride. The result? The overall market for diamond jewelry grew more than 20%, and the market for diamond jewelry designed specifically for weddings increased more than 30%. Most importantly, planning was useful in identifying a situation and mining insights that provoked a cultural shift.

Yoo-Hoo Chocolate Drink

Yoo-hoo chocolate drink had long been suffering from declining sales when it hired the Mad Dogs & Englishmen agency. Quantitative research already had indicated that the brand was seen as old-fashioned, boring, and "not for me." Yoo-hoo is considered part of the soft drink and beverage category, and other drinks in the category (such as Sprite or Minute Maid Juice) were seen as more hip to drink. Moreover, in interviews with mothers (the obvious target market because they generally buy soft drinks for their children), it was found that they would buy the drink for their younger children but not for their teenage children. Teenagers, especially boys, believed that Yoo-hoo was an old-fashioned drink for their little brothers and sisters, not something "adult." Because teenagers consume more soft drinks than any other group, this was a major hurdle and one that needed to be overcome to get the brand back on track. Hence, Mad Dogs & Englishmen's initial recommendation was that Yoo-hoo target teenagers, not their moms ("Mad Dogs & Englishmen: Yoo-hoo Chocolate Drink," 1999).

Mad Dogs & Englishmen's account planning team turned to the Internet for some preliminary research and found that some teenage boys had created webpages glorifying Yoo-hoo. The content of these pages paid homage to Yoo-hoo through such things as testimonials and photo collages. The pages revealed that for these teens, Yoo-hoo represented goodness and the ability to make things right, a calming presence that was in contrast to the edgier advertising messages of more popular soft drinks. Though this web group was small and not representative of how most teens viewed Yoo-hoo, it did give the account planning team an idea of how to position the brand against larger competitors. The insight resulted in the facetious but charming strategy that "Unlike other drinks, Yoo-hoo makes a bad situation better." The sheer irony of the strategy and the joke behind it was a compelling message for teens. The campaign executions showed teens in everyday situations in which the purchase of Yoo-hoo made things better while its absence made things worse. All included the tagline, "Yoo-hoo chocolate drink. Buy any other beverage and you could be making a terrible mistake." As a result of the advertising, the brand's sales decline reversed and its distribution strengthened. Campaign evaluations concluded that the ads were functioning just as the strategy intended.

These are three examples of how research conducted by account planners was used to develop creative strategy leading to successful advertising campaigns. Other notable campaigns in which account planning played a key role include Volkswagen's "Drivers Wanted" campaign, for which planners used one-on-one interviews and focus groups to develop the brand essence of the automobile manufacturer; Norwegian Cruise Line's "It's Different Out Here" campaign, where planners concept tested the main idea through the use of an idea video; and Florida's Anti-Tobacco campaign (which later was rolled out nationally), for which members of the agency team conducted ethnographic and observational research to develop the award-winning "Truth" campaign.

ACCOUNT PLANNING AS PART OF THE OVERALL MARKETING EFFORT

Although the emphasis in this book is on how to use qualitative research to create great advertising, it's important to note that advertising does not exist in a vacuum in today s complex marketing environment. Instead, it plays one role in an often bewildering combination of advertising, sales promotion, public relations, and personal selling. In other words, advertising functions as just one part of the promotion P—the communication mix—that your marketing teacher always talked about when she was discussing the four Ps of marketing (product, price, place, and promotion). To explain this complex promotional recipe, marketers and academics coined the phrase "integrated marketing communications," or IMC. Essentially, the idea behind IMC is that a company speaks to its various publics with a singular voice, one that's closely tied to a brand's identity. In practice, this means that all forms of communication are conveying the same message or image. This consistent messaging leads to a brand personality and helps grow the equity, or value, of a brand. Brand equity, especially in categories with a lot of parity, can mean the difference between a product's success and failure.

The concept of IMC suggests that the strategies and techniques used in account planning extend beyond advertising. Account planning is primarily focused on improving the creative product, but insights generated from planning research can also improve or inform other areas of business strategy. Indeed, for more than a decade, planning's professional associations have been emphasizing the need for it to be integrated into all aspects of the marketing mix: product, price, place, and promotion. And this makes sense: You wouldn't want your advertising centered on building long-term equity in a brand while your sales promotion efforts tell consumers that there's always a coupon available in the Sunday newspaper for 50 cents off the brand. These two things are at odds with each other; while your advertising may be building brand equity, your sales promotion is diluting your brand equity by telling the consumer that your product is always for sale and not worth its full price. Don't get us wrong, we've got nothing against sales promotions; we just want you to really think about what these things say to consumers and the impact they have. Similarly, if your brand's Facebook page gives off a free-form, Grateful Dead sort of vibe but its Twitter account shrieks bluegrass, that's a disconnect. And consumers, astute as they are, notice these differences and become confused.

Unfortunately, it appears that account planning is not as integrated into the marketing process as it might be. A national U.S. survey of account planners that we conducted suggests that although more than 80% of account planners are "very involved" in brand strategy and creative strategy development, less than 6% indicated a high level of involvement in any of the following areas: media strategy development, public relations strategy development, or sales promotion strategy development. We hope that as you read this book, you'll see some areas where the strategies and techniques we describe can be applied to communications campaigns that go beyond traditional advertising.

ORGANIZATION OF THIS BOOK

This chapter serves as an introduction to this book and lays the foundation for explaining the perspective from which we're writing. Below, we briefly discuss what's in store for you in the remaining chapters.

In Chapter 2, we give you an overview of the theory behind qualitative research. We're operating here on the premise that you must understand the underpinnings of qualitative research before you can use it successfully. After all, there are many different research approaches, and it's important for you to decide which approach is the best for getting at what you want to know. Quantitative methods, such as phone surveys, are often used quite successfully in advertising, as are methods such as one-on-one interviews or accompanied shopping. The key to using any research method correctly is knowing its appropriateness for a given situation. We hope our theoretical discussion of qualitative research will help give you an idea of when certain techniques are or are not appropriate.

Chapter 3 deals with ethnographies and other extended-contact methods. We've written this chapter with the following in mind: The best way to get to know a market is to live with that market. Ethnographic and other extended-contact qualitative methods allow researchers to come as close as possible to living with a consumer group by researching that group in its natural setting. However, these methods often require a large time investment. This chapter explores these methods and presents examples of how to conduct such extended-contact research projects as efficiently as possible. Examples illustrating how ethnographic methods have been successfully applied to account planning are incorporated to make the techniques more relevant to planners. The methods explored include ethnography, accompanied shopping, and panel studies with consumers, along with some case studies that illustrate how these techniques have been successfully used in the past. We've also included a discussion on the ethics associated with this type of research.

Our research with account planners suggests that interviewing is their most often used and most valued technique. That's why we spend a lot of time in this book talking about interviewing techniques and how to get the most out of an interview. In Chapter 4, we discuss in great detail interviewing and its utility for account planning. We've also provided a sample transcript from an interview and ideas for how you should approach its analysis.

Account planners have been characterized as creative researchers. They have earned this label because their contributions help generate messages that are creative and resonate with the intended market. The label "creative researcher" also comes from the innovative research techniques used by planners to uncover consumer insights. In Chapter 5, we examine projective and elicitation techniques that may be used by planners to help generate insights into consumer behavior. We give you an overview of the history of projective techniques along with their evolution as tools for market research. Descriptions of some of these techniques, as well as examples of how they can be used by account planners, are provided. These techniques include associations, completions, constructions, expressions, and perceptual mapping. Specific examples, such as the use of role playing, sentence completion, collage building, and other visual prompts (e.g., bubble mapping or games such as "The House Where the Brand Lives") are also provided.

The Internet can be a powerful tool for uncovering consumer insights. Chapter 6 examines how account planners can use the resources and power of the Internet to conduct qualitative research for communication campaigns. The chapter begins with a short history of the Internet as a communications tool and provides an overview of ways the Internet has been used to collect both quantitative and qualitative information. The main focus of the chapter is on describing how the Internet can be used to conduct interviews and online focus groups. We describe the benefits and limitations of both of these methods and also offer tips on how to encourage participation and candidness. Examples are included to illustrate the value of online interviewing for planners. We've also included a discussion of the ethical considerations of doing online qualitative research, including assessments of participant risk, the appropriateness of topics, and obtaining informed consent.

You've done all the research and uncovered some remarkable things. Now, the question is, how do you present the material in a way that will inspire the creative team? Chapter 7 covers two important tasks in the job of an account planner: writing the creative brief and bringing research to life. First, we discuss how account planners can create the most effective written briefs possible. An overriding theme of this section is the use of the creative brief to open creative doors, not close them. The importance of the creative brief is discussed, and we give you an overview of the different types of formats used for developing written briefs. We also address how to fine-tune the brief based on your personal knowledge and your relationship with the creative team. Topics addressed include interpreting the research results in the brief, partnering with creatives to develop briefs, writing a brief that connects with creatives, maintaining focus in the brief, finding trigger words, and allowing for flexibility.

Inspiring research can't inspire if it's not presented in a way that makes the results come to life for the strategy team. Chapter 7 also talks about ways to bring to life key insights from research by exploring how to present research in a way that allows consumers' voices to be heard. Specifically, in addition to numbers, it explores the use of pictures, video, audio, and computer-related technologies to help the creative team hear the consumer in ways that generally do not happen in traditional research presentations.

Throughout the chapters, we explore how best to use and present qualitative research to generate advertising that is creative and resonates with the intended market. In day-to-day business, however, these ideals must often be balanced with real constraints. Chapter 8 deals with some of these constraints and suggests ways to get the most out of research, given different situations. We talk about things such as the pricing of qualitative research, establishing an appropriate timetable for fielding qualitative research, working with data collection teams or field research companies, meeting the expectations of quantitatively oriented management while still getting rich insight, and avoiding the demands of instant analysis.

In Chapter 9, we explore issues associated with evaluating the work of account planners. We discuss the pressure of demonstrating planning's return on investment in a campaign and present various techniques associated with campaign evaluation. In our "parting thoughts" section, we try to inspire you to use the methods we discuss in this book. We use the metaphor of a toolbox to get you excited about actually using the qualitative tools we've talked about, and we talk about being innovative and looking for problems to which you can apply a new research method (providing it's appropriate). We also give you some parting thoughts on the value of teamwork in conducting research and leave you with a brief discussion of how many of the qualitative research methods you'll read about can be used easily to solve a variety of marketing problems. Let's begin.

2

A Qualitative View of the World

THEORY AND DATA ANALYSIS

Just as account supervisors and creative directors seem to live in two separate worlds, researchers who practice primarily quantitative methods, such as surveys and experiments, live in a world very different from that inhabited by qualitative researchers. One is primarily a world of numbers, and the other is primarily a world of words. What one may consider absolutely necessary, the other may consider largely insignificant. Even within the qualitative world, there are differences regarding the mainsprings of human behavior, what is important, and how to demonstrate the validity of research.

It is unusual for one person to be equally skilled in both quantitative and qualitative research or to be equally enthusiastic about the ability of the two approaches to find truth. Although she may be able to appreciate the contributions of the other, deep in her heart, a researcher feels that one approach just seems more naturally correct than the other. Knowing the theoretical foundations on which research techniques are built should improve your abilities as a planner to choose appropriate methods and then to apply those methods to their best advantage. The question of "how many" is best answered by survey research; however, questions about "what" and "how" are best answered by qualitative research approaches. If you want to know how many people are buying a product, sound survey research combined with random sampling techniques can best answer your question. If you want to know what (the symbolic meaning of a product) people are buying or how they are deciding to buy, then qualitative research may best answer your question.

INSIDE THE QUALITATIVE WORLD

Within the academic and professional research worlds, there are a number of research traditions, all of which fall under the broad umbrella term *qualitative research*. You may encounter such terms as *ecological psychology, holistic ethnography, critical ethnography, cognitive anthropology, phenomenology, ethnomethodology, symbolic interactionism, critical inquiry, feminist scholarship,* and *case study.* What separates these traditions can be determined by examining the research tradition from which each comes and the relative amount of attention given to (a) *context* and environment, (b) social and cultural structures, (c) social interaction, (d) individual interpretation, and (e) individual free will. For example, critical inquiry and feminist scholarship assume that meaning and behavior are greatly influenced by exist-ing social structures, and they therefore focus on such things as how perceived gender differences, distribution of wealth and power, and cultural beliefs constrain meaning and define behavior. Ecological psychology assumes that individual environment and context are keys to understanding behavior, and symbolic interactionism assumes that patterns of social interaction are most important. Although these differences do exist, the similarities are much greater, and they are what bind together these different research traditions.

In qualitative research, everyone is allowed to be a theorist; it would not be uncommon to find that in some situations, context and structure are powerful determinants of behavior and that in other situations, individual will and volition are more important. The flexibility of qualitative research is its greatest asset; qualitative researchers feel free to pick and choose from various research tra-ditions and research techniques, depending on the research ques-tion and the research setting. Researchers steeped in quantitative methods, where a step-by-step recipe often guides the conducting of research and where researchers have been instructed not to exercise their own judgment or insight, are ill at ease in the qualitative world. For additional discussion on the ways quantitative and qualitative researchers tend to see the world, see Taylor (1994).

ASSUMPTIONS THAT BIND

Despite their differences of emphasis, almost all qualitative researchers agree on certain assumptions about the nature of human behavior. These assumptions include seeing people as active, interpreting individuals who construct worlds of meanings and act upon the world rather than allowing the world to act upon them.

Active Individuals

Qualitative researchers see the world as made up of active, interpreting individuals forging purposeful lines of action to accomplish everyday life. Individuals take note of the things around them, process or assign meaning to those things, and then plan courses of action. Because meaning arises from within, behavior cannot be understood by seeking external forces and causes. Human beings are not simple responders to stimuli. Rather, they are constantly interpreting what things mean and responding accordingly. Consider the simple case of a person crossing a street. As outside observers, we might note that a person remains stationary until the image of an outstretched hand is replaced by the image of a person crossing the street. Is this a case of an external stimulus determining the person's behavior, or is this a case of the person interpreting objects and then choosing a course of action? A quantitative researcher might regard this as an example of stimulus-response behavior with a conditioned response to the change in images. A qualitative researcher, on the other hand, regards this behavior as an example of meaningful interpretation followed by a purposeful course of action. And how does the qualitative researcher know this? He asks the pedestrian to describe how he accomplished this everyday task of crossing the street.

Worlds of Meaning

At the center of explanations for human behavior is the concept of "meaning." Understand the meaning(s) and you'll understand the behavior, because behavior follows meaning. Meaning may be shared among individuals: Two or more people (or even two cultures) can agree on what something means. Meaning can also be idiosyncratic, or peculiar to one person. Qualitative researchers seek out shared meanings in order to discover patterns of human behavior. An automobile, of course, is not just a means of transportation. It can also be—all at the same time—an expression of self to an individual, an expression of self to others, an investment, a feeling of freedom, a sensory experience, a means of escape, and an expression of concern for others or for the environment.

Meaning is not static; it changes over time and place, within context, and with people. Something you have accomplished may have one meaning for you at the time of the accomplishment; 10 years later, it may have a different meaning. The accomplishment may be more or less important to you. The accomplishment hasn't changed at all, but the meaning of the accomplishment has.

From the Participant's Perspective

In the world of qualitative research, researchers believe that to understand behavior, you must be able to uncover the meaningful objects in people's worlds and understand those objects from the perspective of the people being studied. Any given product may have one meaning for the producer, another for distributors, and yet other meanings for different groups of consumers. What does it mean to buy and use a certain product category? Within the product category, what kinds of meanings do the various brands or offerings have? How do these meanings lead or connect to decisions to buy certain brands and not others? These are the kinds of questions that qualitative researchers attempt to answer.

By asserting that meaning arises from within the person, qualitative researchers deny that meaning can exist in the object. Product consumption and brands have no meanings except for those that consumers are willing to give them. And these meanings are multiple, individual, shifting, contextual, and shared.

By the turn of this century, smoking cigarettes had taken on a very different meaning than it had in the 1950s. Although product improvements may have been made during the last half of the past century, smoking moved collectively in our judgment from socially acceptable to socially and individually irresponsible. Smoking itself did not change; the meanings, the interpretations—the *reality* of smoking—did, and changes in behavior followed.

Multiple Truths

In a qualitative world, no single, determinable truth exists. Instead, there are truths to be found, and these truths are bound by the time, the context, and the individuals who believe them. Often, shared beliefs or shared realities are what constitute truth. That Brand X is the best cleaning product is a truthful statement within the time and context and for the individuals who believe it. That the world is flat was true within the time and context and for the individuals who believed it.

Obviously, the external world does not allow just any interpretation of itself; there are limits, often defined by culture. However, the limit to interpretations is not "1"; it is a much greater number. Suppose at the end of a business lunch, your potential employee took a piece of bread and pushed it in a circular motion about the surface of his dinner plate, soaking up the last juices of the entree, and then proceeded to eat it. This practice, called sopping, would carry a certain meaning in an American restaurant, probably that the candidate possessed few social skills and lacked a basic knowledge of dining etiquette. However, the exact same behavior in a restaurant in France would be seen as perfectly normal and acceptable. Shift the location to many American supper tables and the behavior remains acceptable. Meaning changes with context.

QUALITATIVE WORDS

Within the qualitative research tradition, certain words carry great significance and meaning. In other traditions, the persons who participate in a research study are commonly called *subjects* or *respondents*, suggesting a hierarchical relationship between the researcher and others. Qualitative researchers want to narrow the distance between themselves and others and, therefore, prefer the term *participants* to refer to the individuals who assist by providing information to the researcher.

Theory in qualitative research refers to an organizing scheme for the *data* that places them in orderly patterns and provides meaning and insight into the lives of others. Theory is not posited before data collection; it comes out of the data and is thus referred to as *grounded theory*, because it is grounded in the data (Glaser & Strauss, 1967).

Guesses and suppositions about what the researcher may find are called *working hypotheses* and are altered and revised or cast aside as data collection proceeds.

Triangulation refers to the use of multiple perspectives, multiple methods, multiple research sites, and multiple researchers to understand more fully the object of the investigation. Multiple approaches are always preferred.

THE QUALITATIVE APPROACH

Qualitative researchers begin with *inductive analysis* and then often swing back and forth between inductive and *deductive analyses*. To start inductively means that researchers find objects and attempt to identify and classify them by their characteristics or distinguishing features. An object can be physical, such as a chair; a cultural belief, such as "time is limited"; or a guiding principle, such as "work hard to get ahead." Then the qualitative researcher moves to the next object and compares it with what already has been defined, asking if the new object fits within the category already established or if it demands a new category. The researcher continues in this fashion until all such categories are defined and the relationships that exist between the categories are established.

Assume that you encounter a spherical-shaped object of orange-yellow color. You note that it grows on a tree. It has a puckery skin that you can peel off. The inside is softer, more watery than the outside, and has a pleasing taste. You might label this "tasty sphere." Next, you notice another spherical-shaped object of about the same size resting under the tree. It has a white, leathery skin that can be removed with great difficulty. In fact, the skin appears to have been sewn on. You remove the skin and find yards and yards of string wrapped around a hard center. The center is black, and when you bite it, you discover it is not juicy or soft and has a most unpleasant taste. Is this also an example of a tasty sphere, or are the differences so great as to demand a new category? That depends on the skill of the researcher. Are oranges and baseballs in the same category? Only if we define the category as "spherical-shaped objects." But in this case, shape is not the essence of the category, and we know that because we went beyond a surface-level investigation. One of the tasks for the qualitative researcher is to go beyond surface descriptions to understand the essence of the world as constructed by the participants.

Qualitative researchers want to know the categories of meaning that participants use in everyday life, but discovering them, categorizing them, and charting their relationships is a little more difficult than distinguishing oranges from baseballs.

QUALITATIVE METHODS

Qualitative research methods are diverse and varied. Any method that allows the researcher to capture the worlds of others can be a valid qualitative technique. These methods include observation, participant observation, in-depth interviewing, documents, and record analysis. Qualitative researchers rarely rely on a single method of gathering data because each method brings its own biases.

Participant observation is sometimes regarded as the purest qualitative research technique because it requires the researcher to spend extended time in a participant's natural setting observing and learning how to do things the way the participant does things. Want to know what it's like to work on a production line in a factory? One of the ways to do that is to observe people on the line, listen to them talk about working on the line, and spend some time on the line yourself.

Participant observation is time-consuming and expensive, and in many situations, access to observing can't be negotiated. If you wanted to study what remedies people take when they have headaches, a pure participant observation approach would require you to participate and observe individuals until the onset of a headache. This could take several days or weeks of observation before a participant suffers a headache. A more economical approach—but perhaps a less rich one—would be to conduct interviews with consumers regarding when and how headaches occur, what remedies they take, and whether specific remedies are associated with certain kinds of headaches.

You might also convene a group of known headache sufferers and engage them in a group discussion.

QUALITATIVE DATA

Qualitative researchers eschew structured questionnaires and scaling devices because they present the world as constructed by the researcher. A series of statements drawn from the research literature or previous studies presents a view of reality as collected by the instrument writer. Any qualitative research technique will allow for participants to respond in their own words. Thus, it is possible to present a qualitative survey in which respondents have the opportunity to introduce their worlds, not simply respond to the researcher's view of the world.

Almost anything can count as data in a qualitative study. This includes letters, shopping lists, photographs, memos, diaries, essays, audiotaped and videotaped interviews, and group discussion transcripts. Because the planner is looking for anything that can give him insight into the meaningful worlds of his participants, anything that can do that should be used.

Qualitative researchers prefer to use multiple methods and multiple sources of data because any given method of data collection and analysis carries its own biases and weaknesses. Through triangulation, planners hope to get a fuller or more nearly complete understanding of consumers by drawing from multiple sources of data and using multiple techniques.

ANALYSIS OF QUALITATIVE DATA

Every qualitative researcher is allowed to be his own theorist. Rather than going into a study with a theory to be tested, qualitative researchers try to enter the worlds of others without any presuppositions about what they might find. Doing qualitative research requires planners to set aside their own personal biases and be fully open to understanding the world as constructed by others.

Assume that your agency has a federal contract to investigate why teenage mothers on welfare continue to have additional children, and it's up to your agency to develop message strategies that would encourage teen mothers not to have additional children.

Your job as a qualitative researcher is neither to pass judgment on your participants nor to inject your own personal opinions as to why this happens. Your goal is to enter into the world of teen mothers (through observation, interviews, participation, etc.) and to understand the meaning of "children" as the teen mothers construct it. You might have a number of working hypotheses that initially guide your collection of data, but you'll most likely discard or alter these as you begin to collect data. For example, you might wonder beforehand whether teen mothers have additional children

- because they are not knowledgeable about their bodies and birth control methods,
- as a way of trying to maintain a relationship with a partner who may provide financially for the children,
- as a way of gaining additional welfare dollars for their families,
- as a way of increasing their status within the community in which they live, or
- because of peer and social pressures that encourage procreation during the teen years.

Each of these five working hypotheses may offer no explanation, a partial explanation, or (rarely is this the case) the complete explanation. Getting at the meaning of additional children to these mothers requires that you understand the world in which they live as they understand it so that message strategies or programs discouraging a behavior can be developed. Your own personal biases and opinions are of no value here—unless, of course, you have a history of being an unwed teenage mother on welfare. Then your own personal experience and insight can be extremely valuable to you. However, planners should never assume that because they are also members of the group being studied that their experiences are the same. No two people have exactly the same experience and, thus, don't understand the world in exactly the same way.

The basic question for most qualitative researchers is, "What is going on here?" Any method of inquiry and any method of data analysis that can help answer that question should be considered an acceptable one. Naturally, there is rarely, if ever, just one thing going on. Human behavior is highly complex, and more commonly, the planner will find that multiple things are happening. For example, the question, "What is going on inside the supermarket?" has multiple answers. In fact, the number of answers to what is going on is probably equal to or greater than the number of people inside the supermarket. Some people are at the cash register, scanning packages, taking other people's money, or putting their purchases in bags. Other people are pushing carts, pausing temporarily at different locations, and then deciding whether to place certain items in the cart—sometimes putting items in and then taking them out of the cart and putting them back on the shelf. Some people have lists of items that they consult frequently, and others have no list at all. Some people have many items in their carts, and when the cart is full, they stand in one kind of line. Others seem to have only a few items that they carry in their hands, and they stand in another kind of line. Yet other people are placing items on the shelves, and others are handing out product samples. If we asked the persons mentioned what they were doing, we would probably get answers such as shopping for the week, dropping in after work, running in and out, checking out, waiting, checking people out, bagging, restocking, and sampling—all of which are part of a smooth-flowing supermarket operation.

Because they enter the world of others without preconceived notions about how things are, qualitative researchers often use the term *sensitized concept* rather than *theory*. Grounded theory (Glaser & Strauss, 1967) means that any explanation you have is grounded in and comes out of the data, not before data are collected. A sensitized concept is one that's sensitive to and comes out of the data. Common everyday sayings such as "It's not what you know, but who you know" and "Who you are determines the quality of service you get" are in fact theories about how the social world works, grounded in people's everyday experiences.

Coding Paradigms

No two researchers will approach data analysis in exactly the same way. Some planners prefer to do the analysis by hand, working from paper copies of transcripts that they mark up, cut up, rearrange, and put back together in various ways. Other planners prefer to work at a computer, inserting word codes, highlighting texts, inserting comments, and so forth, using a simple word processing program. Still others prefer to use a specialized computer program.

Coding data and using coding paradigms are two ways of reducing data to manageable and meaningful units. Keep in mind that data analysis and coding should begin at the same time as data collection. In survey research, all the data are collected, usually entered into a data analysis program, and then analyzed.

In qualitative research, data collection and tentative analysis occur simultaneously. If you wait until all your transcripts are complete and then try to begin analysis, you will have created an almost unmanageable task for yourself.

Analysis itself can be a long, demanding process. Most researchers will swing back and forth between data collection and data analysis as they complete the research assignment. In fact, your own understanding of the *phenomenon* you're studying tells you when it is time to stop collecting data.

Strauss and Corbin (1998) suggest a coding paradigm that consists of coding data into (a) the phenomenon, (b) conditions, (c) actions/interactions, and (d) consequences. The phenomenon is a repeated pattern of behavior and commonly is the behavior you're trying to understand. A condition is a complex set of events that lead up to the phenomenon. Actions/interactions represent the ways people respond to the phenomenon (or the strategies they use). Consequences represent the end result of the actions/interactions. This coding paradigm is particularly useful when coding for a process, such as decision making. Planners often assume that "buying" or "decisions to buy" are the central phenomena of their studies. When this is the case, the planner might examine the data looking for (a) conditions that lead to purchase (e.g., natural depletion, wearing out, running out, acute need, emergencies), (b) actions/interactions involved in the buying decision (e.g., gathering information, making price comparisons, asking a friend, looking for information on the World Wide Web, visiting a retail location), and (c) consequences (e.g., satisfaction, dissatisfaction, unexpected benefits, repeat purchase, depleting the savings account, prideful ownership).

Using a coding paradigm created by others can be handy in the initial coding stages because it makes you look at the data in different ways and may allow you to see relationships within the data that are not obvious. The Strauss and Corbin paradigm is especially helpful when coding for process and when coding for the duality of structural features (often the conditions) and action.

However, planners should not be reluctant to develop their own coding paradigms. Some researchers, for example, are content to code for major themes or trends in the data without charting the relationships among the themes. For example, a study of the current buying patterns among teenagers might include fashion trends, eating-out patterns, musical tastes, activities with friends, and part-time work. There may or may not be a relationship among the various themes (a pure qualitative researcher will believe there is!), and only one or two dominant themes may be of interest to the client. In such cases, the planner may be satisfied to stop with a thematic analysis.

Still other planners may wish to do a metaphorical analysis of the words that participants use. *Metaphors* take the characteristics of one thing and associate them with something entirely different; they are powerful ways of making intangible concepts more tangible. By talking about a thing in terms of something else in an effort to make it more comprehensible, metaphors can be used to provide powerful insight into how people think of themselves and how they behave (Felton, 1994). Consider this quote from a corporate trainer:

> I just can't seem to get through everything I need to in the time we have. There're always so many people interrupting me with questions and making me lose my place. I'm very frustrated with not being able to finish the training session on time.

To code for metaphors, we ask how the language and expressions used by the participant reflect other figures or jobs. The participant says he "can't get through . . . on time," "interrupting me," "losing my place," "not able to finish on time." Obviously, the trainer sees himself as someone who must adhere to a fixed time schedule, have no interruptions, maintain a train of thought, and finish on time. Metaphorically, the participant's language is based in transportation. More listening on our part might help establish the means of transportation: Is he an Amtrak engineer speeding down the train(er's) track? An airline pilot on his way from New York to Los Angeles? A captain of a cruise ship? These types of insights into how people see themselves can help us understand their worlds.

Metaphors exist within the language but slightly below the surface level. Most are usually not visible to the persons who speak them. Nonetheless, they sometimes pop out at the planner and can be a useful analytical tool.

Getting It Right

If human behavior is as complicated as qualitative researchers believe, how is the planner ever to know if she has gotten it right? Unfortunately, no simple test or assessment can confirm the validity of an interpretation. However, there are some procedures and safeguards that planners can use to reduce the chances that they got it wrong.

First, planners have to accept that producing an interpretation of people's behavior that is a verisimilitude, or exact copy, of human behavior is impossible. The best you can produce is a reasonable interpretation that appears to explain the behavior. Before entering a research setting, planners should ask themselves (through working hypotheses) what they think is going on. If the answer after the research is the same as before, the planner has probably gotten it wrong: Rather than discovering a pattern of behavior, the planner has imposed her own interpretation on the data. Keeping track of your own personal biases, prejudices, and opinions before and during the research process helps guard against their overly influencing your interpretation of the data. Writing these down beforehand is a good idea.

During the data collection and temporary analysis of data, planners can write memos or notes to themselves, expressing their initial reactions and conclusions. Tracking these during the research process can help you determine if you have come to understand others or if you have imposed your own interpretations on the data.

Asking a colleague or team member to determine if your interpretations are reasonable based on her examination of some of the transcripts and your coding scheme is another way to guard against personal bias. Particularly in a team research situation, all members must come to a shared understanding of what the data mean.

Yet another way to guard against personal bias is to take your interpretations back to your participants and ask them if they agree. In the process of analysis, you should write summaries of your thoughts on the interviews you're conducting. Ask the participants to read the summaries of their interviews to see if your interpretation matches the participant's perspective.

In the final analysis, it's not so much whether you understood all the behavior you may have observed or listened to people talk about but whether you have a sufficient understanding to speak to the client on behalf of your research participants. Can you provide a reasonable description of the world of the people you have studied from their perspective(s)? If so, you have accomplished your research task as a planner.

MULTIPLE VERSUS MIXED METHODS

In recent years, there has been a movement within research communities to mix methods on research projects—that is, to combine survey research with, for example, interviews. Quantitative researchers sometimes refer to this mixing of methods as "adding qualitative flesh to quantitative bones."

From a theoretical view, the qualitative paradigm and the quantitative paradigm do not "mix" well. Most mixed-methods studies are driven by the assumptions underlying quantitative research, not qualitative research. Quantitative research is conducted from the point of view of the researcher, not from that of the participant. Quantitative research advocates an external truth knowable to the researcher and not to the participant. In quantitative research, "what people say" is generally irrelevant; in qualitative, it is the essence of the approach. Thus, the underlying assumptions driving the two approaches are seen as contradictory.

This is not to argue that advocates from one approach cannot learn from and borrow techniques from the other. Suppose, for example, you have conducted long interviews with individuals about a procedure being introduced in a workplace. Let's say the procedure is a new electronic surveillance system used to record whether healthcare workers are following prescribed guidelines for washing their hands before touching hospital patients. Such an introduction is likely to induce strong reactions. From your interviews, you might draw a number of positive and negative statements, create a degree-of-agreement scale, and administer the scale to all the workers falling under the guidelines to get some sense of the distribution of opinions. In doing so, you have maintained the perspectives of the participants while gauging the depth of agreement among the larger population. Generally, long interviews of 10 to 15 participants are sufficient to uncover the range of meanings associated with a particular phenomenon within a shared culture. If you had derived a scale based on your own understanding of the phenomenon or based on published research, you would have failed to capture the "from the participants' perspectives" aspect so critical to conducting good qualitative research. If you want to understand, and ultimately change, human behavior, you must understand the meanings of the things that lead to the behavior.

Certainly, survey researchers can add understanding to their findings by interviewing some respondents, but the boundaries of the understanding are predetermined by the survey questions. If you ever have been asked to fill out a questionnaire and found that none of the available response categories matched what you thought, you have encountered the setting of the boundaries of meaning by someone else.

Qualitative researchers often use purposive sampling, where persons to be interviewed are chosen for a particular reason related to the study, such as growing up in a one-parent household; being a high school dropout; or being a brand-loyal, heavy user of a product. When no clear logic exists for choosing the sample, then generating a small random sample from a list of the universe, just as quantitative researchers do, makes good sense.

Qualitative research is always made stronger by the use of multiple methods, multiple perspectives, and multiple researchers. If data collected from individual interviews, document analysis, participant observation, and group discussions all point to the same meanings, then the researcher can be confident that she has found something meaningful in the lives of the participants. This use of multiple methods within the qualitative set of assumptions is called triangulation.

If you are asked to join a mixed-methods research team as a qualitative researcher, clarify your role in advance. Will you be asked to "add flesh to quantitative bones"—essentially using a qualitative method to add explanation to quantitative findings? Or will you be asked to design a qualitative study from the ground up? Attempting to "add flesh" is not nearly as challenging as designing a plan to uncover the essence of the phenomenon.

SUMMARY

Qualitative researchers see individuals as active, interpreting beings who construct worlds of meaning and act upon the world rather than allowing the world to act upon them. Qualitative research seeks to see and understand the world from the perspective of the people being studied.

Meaning is a central concept in qualitative studies because meaning and interpretation guide behavior. Meaning is said to be multiple, changing, and dependent on context and time.

Qualitative researchers prefer to use multiple research methods because of the inherent bias in any given method. Data can be analyzed in a variety of ways, including process analysis, thematic analysis, and metaphorical analysis.

Researchers guard against personal bias in their interpretations of human behavior by articulating their own biases before the research begins, tracking their interpretations as they change, asking colleagues to review their interpretations, and sharing their interpretations with their participants.

Qualitative research turns many of the so-called standard research procedures upside down. Getting close to consumers, making them partners in the research process, and massaging data are not research crimes within the qualitative research traditions. The following chapter on ethnographic methods reveals some ways to get close to your consumers so you can understand them better.

KEY TERMS

context: The surroundings or environment in which a phenomenon occurs. Context changes the meaning of the phenomenon.

data: Anything created or changed by humans that gives the researcher insight into how the participants construct their realities.

deductive analysis: Procedure that begins with a broad, general statement about relationships you hope to find.

grounded theory: Theory that is grounded in the data.

inductive analysis: Procedure that begins with focusing on a single observation.

metaphor: A way of understanding the essence of something not well understood by comparing it to something more readily understood.

participants: People from whom the researcher gathers information.

phenomenon: Something that becomes the central focus of a research study, often not obvious at the beginning of a qualitative study.

reality: What is perceived to be true by an individual or by groups of individuals. Reality exists within the meaning structures created by the individuals and not in the objects of the physical world. Reality is not static; it changes across time, space, context, and with individuals.

sensitized concept: A concept sensitive to the data that helps explain relationships found in the data.

theory: The organizing scheme that helps you make sense of your data. It grows out of the analytical process; it is not posited before.

triangulation: Using more than one method or perspective in a qualitative study. A researcher could triangulate interviews and text analysis or thematic analysis and metaphorical analysis. The assumption is that if two sets of data or two types of analysis suggest the same thing, then the researcher can have greater confidence in the findings.

working hypothesis: A researcher's hunch about what he or she may find. Hypotheses are discarded or changed as additional data support or fail to support them.

EXERCISES

1.   Talk to 8 or 10 of your friends about their favorite item of clothing. Ask them to talk about how they acquired it, how long they have had it, where and when they wear it, and what makes it special to them. What insights can you draw from the conversations about the meaning of clothes? Is the meaning in the item or in the person? Can you find instances where interaction with others has reinforced or changed the meaning? Are there differences in your understanding between participants who were wearing or able to show you the item compared with those who could only describe it? Does the context in which the person wears the item change the meaning in any way? How can these insights be used to develop message strategy for (a) a laundry detergent that claims to work gently on colors and fibers, (b) a dry cleaning business, (c) a clothing alteration business, or (d) the introduction of a vintage line of clothing?

2.   Ask several people to tell you about items they have inherited (or hope to inherit) from a relative. Ask them to tell you about what they think the item meant to the relative and what it means to them. How has the relative's owning the item influenced the meaning of the item for the person who now owns it?

3.   Ask separately a male friend and a female friend to talk to you about how they have celebrated Valentine's Day over the years. How does the meaning of this holiday change over time? How do you think the meaning of this holiday differs between genders as well as within genders? Why don't all men or all women feel the same way?

4. A quantitative study of hand-washing practices among healthcare workers concluded that healthcare workers did not wash their hands as often as they should because there were not enough wash stations. Why do you think adding more wash stations did not improve the rate?

RELATED READING

Denzin, N., & Lincoln, Y. (Eds.). (2005). *Handbook of qualitative research* (3rd ed.). Thousand Oaks, CA: Sage.

Glaser, B., & Strauss, A. (1967). *The discovery of grounded theory*. Chicago, IL: Aldine.

Taylor, S. J., & Bogdan, R. C. (1984). *Introduction to qualitative research methods: The search for meanings* (2nd ed.). New York, NY: Wiley.

3

Ethnographic Methods for Advertising Research

Before we dive into methods, we need to get a handle on the term *ethnography*. *Ethnos* is a Greek term that denotes a people, race, or cultural group (Smith, 1989). Ethnography is the study of people and the cultures they create. It is a branch of descriptive anthropology devoted to describing ways of life and humankind (Vidich & Lyman, 2000). This sounds a lot like what planners do. In fact, we think of planners as ethnographers. Our job is to be constantly curious about ways of life and humankind. We have to understand people and the culture within which they live. This culture is the context in which our brand, message, and media strategies must *resonate*.

GETTING EMIC

There are two general traditions of ethnographic analyses: etic and emic. *Etic* analyses are views of a culture from outside the culture.

In *Why We Buy: The Science of Shopping,* Paco Underhill (2000) describes many etic methods of studying shopping behavior. For example, trailing shoppers is one such method his researchers employ. Trailing involves following shoppers and taking notes about their behavior without being noticed by them. Certainly, you can learn a great deal about behavior from watching. However, what you miss from just watching is how individuals make sense of what they are doing. Underhill comments,

> In addition to measuring and counting every significant motion of a shopping trip, the trackers must also contribute incisive field notes describing the nuances of customer behavior, making intelligent inferences based on what they've observed. (p. 15)

Making such inferences on behalf of your subjects is what an etic analysis is. An etic ethnographic analysis amounts to our interpretation of another's culture.

There is one major pitfall of etic analysis. Consider our researcher stumbling on a strange custom among a strange people. She deduces that this must be some type of tribal mating dance. After all, each person from the strange culture she is observing engages in a similar dance when passing by the observation point, and both genders are present when this strange motion occurs. But without stopping to ask the participants what's going on, she won't know that this dance is really the result of bare feet on hot pavement.

The second type of ethnographic analysis is *emic* analysis, or analysis of a culture from within the culture. Emic analysis more closely matches our perspective on qualitative research. Because culture is created by the participants, we feel it is vitally important to understand the culture as the participants understand it. Also, our marketing messages must resonate within our participants' culture. Resonance happens when we strike a chord in consumers—when we make them see our products or services in a way that is meaningful in their lives. Resonance happens in the brains of our participants. All these ideas require research methods that give us access to our participants' thoughts and feelings so we can understand how they create their worlds.

Ethnographies are holistic and attempt to examine a wide variety of ways in which people express the meaning of the culture they are creating. Expressions of meaning can be words, music, literature, diaries, art, dance, mode of dress, construction of personal space, construction of workspace, home decor, architecture and placement of buildings, and so on. Thus, ethnographies usually consist of a variety of data-gathering techniques. They also can be time and cost intensive if done exhaustively.

The good news is that you don't necessarily have to execute a full-blown ethnography to generate ethnographic insights. In fact, many times, getting quality ethnographic insights doesn't have to cost a lot of money at all. This chapter explores a few ethnographic methods that can help planners see how people understand the world around them.

PARTICIPANT OBSERVATION

Just about any study that involves humans can be called an observational study. However, *participant observation* studies require us as researchers to participate to some degree in the thing we are studying. Participant observation is a core ethnographic technique, and it's an active technique. It happens in the everyday environment of our consumers. It's a way to experience our consumers' lives firsthand.

Not all subjects can be studied using participant observation. Sometimes, topics are too private. We probably wouldn't get too far as participant observers trying to research condom use. Sometimes, there is nothing to observe about the topic in which we are interested. For example, if we want to understand how people make sense of social issues, such as advertising potentially harmful products to minors, finding something to observe that answers our question is difficult. Other times, the context within which the action happens may be unsafe. For example, you want to understand the culture of inner-city gangs but may not be comfortable participating in their activities.

So what types of topics lend themselves to participant observation? Activities work well for participant observation. One Tennessee-based, planning-driven advertising agency used participant observation to understand the meaning of a state park. Their researchers went camping, sharing the experience of the great outdoors with people who were using the state parks. Want to know how international tourists experience a U.S. amusement park? We did, and we joined a tour bus of French visitors in Orlando, Florida, spending multiple days with them as we all went on vacation. How do people really make a car-buying decision? Find out by going car shopping with prospective buyers.

A major advantage of participant observation is that you get fresh impressions, right as things are happening. You can also see how the experience evolves, how impressions change, how people navigate a situation, and how they relate to others in that situation. With follow-up discussions, you can see how people reflect on their experience and make sense of it.

Let's Go Shopping

A useful participant observation tool for understanding how people make sense of retail environments is *accompanied shopping*—that is, going shopping with consumers. What you do during an accompanied shopping experience depends on the goal of your study. For example, let's say your client is Abercrombie & Fitch (A&F). A&F was worried that too many younger teens were buying its clothes, which was making it "uncool" with its core market, college-aged young people. As a brand strategy, A&F launched a new line of stores under a different name (Hollister), directed to younger teens. In developing these stores, A&F needed to understand how teens approach the retail environment as well as its specific store. Well, if you've spent any time in a suburban shopping mall, you know teens don't just shop in a mall; they seem to live there—at least during the summer. So what does going to the mall mean to teens? What does buying clothing mean to teens? Well, hang out and do the mall with them. Try to understand how teens make sense of shopping at the new store in the context of the larger experience of going to the mall.

If you were representing a client who markets compact discs, then you would want to go disc shopping with defined types of buyers (e.g., heavy users, medium users, light users). You would probably go to at least two places where your individual subject reports buying CDs. This would allow you to have the participant compare retail environments for you. You can also see how your shoppers navigate a store, what sections they go to first, how they search for CDs, if they use the listening bars, and so on. In addition, you can gather thoughts and feelings while the activity is in progress.

Accompanied shopping is an interview on the move. For our disc buyer, we might ask questions such as, What is your impression of this store? Where would you start your search? How do you decide what to look for? What is it like to shop here? Sometimes, projective types of questions can be fun and insightful— for example, If this store were a person, what would that person be like? (We discuss projective techniques in detail later, in Chapter 5.)

If possible, we would want to record the conversation, which means we need a small portable recorder, a remote microphone, a notepad, and good ears. Taking photos can also be useful if the store will allow that. Sometimes recording isn't possible. That means you need those good ears and an even better memory. Whether you can record while moving or not, build in time for a discussion over coffee or a soda after the shopping experience and have the participant reflect on his day with you. Recording and note taking may be easier in this environment.

Hint: Before charging into a retail store with a recording device, camera, and notepad in hand, you may want to fill in the store manager on what you're up to. Otherwise, you might find yourself being chased from the store by a large, unsympathetic security guard.

GENERAL ISSUES WITH PARTICIPANT OBSERVATION STUDIES

Once you've found a topic that lends itself to participant observation, you may need to ask yourself how far you're willing to participate. Your European swimsuit client may be important to your agency, but are you willing to prance on the beach in a teeny-weeny swath of cloth in order to understand the experience of using the product? The good news is that you can understand culture without *going native*, or becoming a full participant in the culture. In fact, keeping a bit of distance while in the context of what you are studying can help you see things you might miss if you are immersed in the culture. Instead of actually being European swimsuit wearers, we can gain emic insight into the culture by spending time at the beach, watching interactions between the swimsuit wearers and observers, talking with European swimsuit wearers about the experience of wearing the suits, getting to know the users, gaining access to see what their lives are like, listening to their conversations, engaging them in interviews about things specific to our client's products, gaining valuable insights, and avoiding personal overexposure!

Gaining Access and Building Trust

Perhaps the two most important steps in fielding an ethnographic study are *gaining access* to the context you want to study and building trust with your participants. The more public the space in which the phenomenon happens, the easier it is to gain access to it. For example, understanding fan behavior at a sporting event is relatively easy in terms of access. Getting behind the doors of a business to observe how businesspeople make use of technology in the workplace can be a bit more difficult. Getting into homes, as the Richard's Group did when doing primary ethnographic research for Thomasville Furniture (American Association of Advertising Agencies, 2008, p. 75), can be most difficult. Each context requires you to seek permission from different people.

In all cases, we'd recommend that you get permission from your participants. They will want to know why you're around, so you should be upfront about your purpose. Honesty from you is more likely to result in honesty from them than if they are suspicious of your presence. For businesses, you'll need to find out who in the business can give you permission to get in the door. It may be useful to have that person show you around the business setting and introduce you to people to give you more credibility with your participants.

ETHICS BOX 1: DO YOU HAVE A RIGHT TO KNOW YOU'RE BEING STUDIED?

How would you feel if you found out someone was secretly studying your behavior? How would you feel about the brand that person was representing? What are the possible ramifications of secretly studying people? Do you think people have the ethical right to know they are being studied? We'll give you our answers to this dilemma later in this chapter, but for now, what do you think?

One way to gain access is to go into situations where you have existing contacts. If people know you already and know that you're reputable, you will have an easier time of gaining access. In situations where you do not have existing contacts, use of others who do have contacts is often essential. For example, in a study to develop HIV/AIDS education and prevention strategies for young adults living in rural areas, a team of "city-slicker" researchers was faced with the task of gaining access to the everyday lives of rural young adults. We did not know anyone in the target market who lived in the areas we were studying, and we could not find researchers anywhere with contacts in this market. We spent the first few days of the study just exploring the area, looking at businesses, finding out where the schools and churches were, listening to local radio, reading the local newspaper, and just trying to figure out what people did in this area. We knew we needed some local people who would buy into our research project, who were knowledgeable about people living in the area who fit our target market, and whom people in the area trusted. We hoped these key people would vouch for us with the locals to help us gain access.

While driving around, we noticed there was only one pharmacy in town. The mental wheels started turning. We thought that just about everyone in a small town would need a prescription filled at some point, and this town was small enough that a local pharmacist would likely know many, many people. A pharmacist would be sympathetic to research aimed at a public health issue. Plus, people would likely trust the pharmacist. We knew we had it! But to be on the safe side, we stopped several places and told people we needed to fill a prescription. We asked folks where we should go and if they thought the pharmacist would be helpful. Fortunately, everyone we asked seemed to have a great deal of respect for the husband and wife pharmacists who ran the local shop. We drove straight to the pharmacy. After talking with the pharmacists for just a few minutes, we knew we had, indeed, hit it. They invited us to their home that evening, fed us, and we talked about the project. Immediately, they began to help us identify people to use in the study, made contacts for us, and told folks that we were OK.

Having someone to vouch for you is helpful in gaining trust. However, the burden of gaining trust eventually falls on your shoulders. You have to look and sound credible but not threatening. In terms of looking credible, think about your audience. If you need to speak with corporate executives, you'd better look like an executive. If you're talking to young adults, blue jeans may be the ticket to reducing barriers between you and your participants. In terms of sounding credible but not threatening, we've found two techniques that work well. First, let your participants know what you are doing and why. Explain to them that there are no right or wrong answers. Tell them you are there to learn from them. Stress that they are the experts, not you.

The second way to put your participants at ease is to have them talk about the one thing they know best: themselves. Ask them to explain their daily routine to you. The amount of time you spend engaged in this type of conversation depends on the type of person with whom you are talking. The *rapport*-building stage is important with executives, but because their time is valuable, you may want to do less of this. If people seem really uncomfortable with you, then you may need to spend more time on this activity.

A word of caution: Unless you're an Oscar-winning actor, don't try to be someone you're not. This is especially important with kids. Kids know you're not a kid. You will likely come across as pretty goofy if you try to act too much like a kid. Just be yourself. After all, that's what you're asking your participants to do, so why not set a good example?

Finding Participants

One strength of ethnographic methods is emergent design. *Emergent design* means that we can change the research methodology in the field if we find we are barking up the wrong tree or if we find aspects of the culture we haven't yet considered. Randomized participant selection isn't a goal. Rather, pushing for diversity of perspectives regarding the culture you are interested in is a more appropriate goal. In our HIV/AIDS study, once we gained access to a few young adults, we used them to direct us to other types of people who might be similar to or different from them. This technique of using current participants to recruit additional participants is called *snowballing* and is a useful emerging design tool. We listened to how the young adults described the different types of young people who lived in the community, then asked them to put us in touch with other young people who fit in the various categories they had described.

During the ongoing recruiting process, constantly ask yourself, "Whose perspective are we missing?" In our HIV/AIDS study, we expanded our sample to include school administrators, teachers, preachers, preachers' wives, some parents, and so on, and we thought we had it all wrapped up. Then we had a stroke of luck that we couldn't have anticipated. After being stood up for an interview session (which will sometimes happen to the best of us), we wandered around a park in the downtown area of the little town. It was midmorning on Saturday, and we noticed a group of young adults cleaning up the park. We walked over, struck up a conversation, and found that these young folks were doing community service for various legal offenses. We asked a few if they would talk with us after they were done. Dumb luck led us to an entirely different side of this rural area, a side that our other helpers were not familiar with. Among these young people were folks who represented high school dropouts and who largely fell within a lower socioeconomic category. In fact, upon further discussion with our medical advisors on the study, we learned that women in this particular group are most at risk for HIV infection. We had located what was perhaps the most critical population to find by being in the field, keeping our eyes open, and asking questions.

You may have noticed that we did not use the term *sample* when talking about our research participants. That term has strong quantitative research connotations and may lead your clients to evaluate your work based on criteria that are inappropriate for your research goal. For example, *sample* usually brings to mind random selection of subjects based on the criterion of statistical generalizability. *Convenience sample* often leads people to feel that your participant selection was somehow compromised, or that you settled on a nonrandom sample because of "convenience" rather than research rigor.

In qualitative research, our goal is to find the right people who have access to the phenomenon we're studying. We don't bow to the constraints of statistical convention. We are not trying to measure indices of a phenomenon, then infer about that phenomenon based on measurements. Rather, we go right to the heart of the phenomenon, which for us is meaning. We explore meaning, not from measures that we as researchers create but through the languages our participants use to construct and express meaning and the ways they do so. Therefore, our need for participants is different.

Finding the right participants means identifying people who can best illuminate the phenomenon we need to understand. Consider this problem: You want to understand the experience of college students getting into credit card trouble. Can just any college student relay this experience to you? What does it mean to "get into credit card trouble"? Should you define a debt amount in advance (e.g., a college student is in credit card trouble if she has X amount of dollars in credit card debt)? Well, that depends on how rich that student is, doesn't it? What about saying a student is in credit card trouble if he makes only the minimum payment amount each month? Or if she skips payments altogether? Also, how often does a person know when he is actually getting into trouble? Maybe the student feels he is handling his credit card balances just fine despite the fact that he owes several thousand dollars. So who can best help us understand the experience of getting into credit card trouble?

This is a case where finding the right participants is critical. One solution is to find those students who already have recognized that they are in credit card trouble. In this case, hindsight is better. We would want to ask how they discovered they were in credit card trouble, what credit card trouble means for them, how they got into that situation in the first place, what it's like to be in trouble and what they need in order to get out of trouble, and so on. Because they've realized they are in trouble, these particular college students can better see the events and behaviors that led to their current lot. In this case, we didn't need all college students, only the right college students.

What Should You Be Looking For?

What you're looking for in an ethnographic study depends on the research questions. At the very least, to get an emic understanding of the culture, you're going to need interview data. We devote an entire chapter to interviewing later in this book. Beyond that, think about how you're going to bring this culture to life for your client, account team, media planners, and creatives. As a planner, you're lucky. You get to experience this wonderful, rich experience firsthand. Now you have to convey this experience to others. Here are some things you can do:

- Take photos of your participants so your agency and client can put faces to research results.
- Take photos of your participants' homes, workplaces, and so on.
- Ask your participants to help you make a photo essay of a particular experience, such as being in a state park.
- Ask your participants to help you make a video essay of an experience.
- Ask your participants to keep a diary of their experiences with you.
- Make note of the music, television, films, books, and more that are popular with your participants.
- Whenever possible, use your participants' own words to describe their experiences.

Let others see your participants' faces and hear their voices. After all, your participants are the experts here. You're the medium. (We talk more in Chapter 7 about presenting your research insights.)

How Do You Know When You've Recruited Enough Participants?

In ethnographic investigations, as in other types of qualitative studies, data collection and data analysis happen concurrently. If you're not reflecting on the data you are collecting, you cannot know where to go next in the field. You know you have enough participants when you've pushed for diversity among your sample and you're confident that you're hearing the same variety of perspectives over and over. This is called reaching *information saturation* or *data redundancy*.

Building Trust and the Observer Effect

No matter what type of research you do, you can't avoid impacting the phenomenon. What you can do is try to lessen your impact on the phenomenon. In participant observation, time and trust can reduce the *observer effect*. That is, people are likely to act differently if they know they are being observed. However, over time and as your research subjects' comfort level with you rises, more usual behavior tends to emerge.

Some researchers may argue that you can totally overcome the observer effect by going *covertly* into the research setting. We have major ethical problems with this idea. First, we firmly believe people have the right to know their behavior is being monitored. Also, there is a major risk to your monetary and time investment in the study if you are found out. That is, if people feel their trust has been violated, they are likely to withdraw from you and not give you access to the information you need. Let's face it: Without people to research, you can't generate emic understandings to guide your strategy. Finally, with skill and patience, the observer effect can be effectively minimized, thus allowing honest flow of information from your participants.

Exiting the Field

By the end of an ethnographic study, you may have spent a great deal of time with your participants. Thinking about how you are going to exit the research setting is important for several reasons. First, you may find the need to reenter the setting later, so leaving on good terms is essential. Second, you're dealing with human beings who have given you their time and bared their souls to you. What have you given them? Of course, in many of our research initiatives, we depend on monetary compensation to help recruit participants. Although money helps, there are some nonmonetary ways to compensate participants for their efforts. For example, depending on the constraints of the study, *debriefing* your participants on what you've found out in the study can provide a sense of closure. Your participants are likely to be curious about what you've discovered, and a debriefing can also show them how they've contributed to your knowledge. Also, a debriefing can be a good *validity* check for your analysis. If you're getting curious looks from your participants as you tell them all about their culture, you probably need to ask some more questions. On the other hand, laughs of recognition can send you home from the field with confidence that you've done a decent job of capturing these people's experiences.

Sometimes, depending on your topic, you may feel a greater need to give back to your participants. In the HIV/AIDS study we've been discussing, it was apparent that many of our participants held beliefs and were engaged in situations that put them at risk of contracting the virus. They could have interpreted our silence as validation that they were safe. To satisfy what we felt was our ethical duty, once their participation concluded, we gave participants leaflets about HIV and AIDS as well as phone numbers they could call for help.

ETHICS BOX 2: BEER BRAND RESEARCH— WHAT WOULD YOU DO?

As we did in our HIV/AIDS study, you may find unanticipated situations when doing qualitative research, such as misunderstandings about health. In the case of health behaviors, it seems pretty clear that providing some additional information to your participants after the data collection, to clear up misunderstandings or to help them make better decisions, is the right thing to do. But consider this scenario.

You are researching perceptions and use of beer brands among young adults. However, the interviews reveal that your client's brand is considered to be the best brand for underage binge drinking. What should you do? Why? Is this any of your business? Do you have any obligation to the client to tell them? What if doing something about this hurts your client's beer sales? Do you have any obligation to those who might be abusing the product (i.e., binge drinking)? Where does your ethical obligation as a researcher/strategist start and stop?

PANEL STUDIES

Many times, you can't afford the time or money required for an extended in-field ethnographic experience. Panel studies can be a solution for this. A *panel study* involves recruiting a group of people and tracking them over time using a variety of techniques. You can schedule individual or group interviews at various intervals over a specified period of time. Between interview sessions, you can have your participants keep diaries, take photos, or make videos of the experience you are exploring. Sometimes, you can use cell phone (or other personal electronic device) or Internet technology to keep track of what's going on. We'll go into greater detail about using Internet technology in the field in Chapter 6.

Launching the Steam N' Clean

Panel studies can be useful when you are launching a new product. For example, Erich Pagel, the marketing research director for the Bissell Cleaning Products company, developed a successful strategy for a new product launch from a meager $1,500 investment in ethnographic research using a panel design.

Because Bissell had an established record with other cleaning products, they knew that women and children were heavy users of their products. With limited time and money, Pagel looked for an organization where women with children could be found. The local Parent Teacher Association (PTA) proved to be a great answer to his problem. In return for a $1,500 donation to the organization, Pagel was allowed to give a presentation to the PTA and recruited 20 PTA moms to try the new Bissell product in their homes. The moms kept *diaries* of their experiences using the product over a 2- to 3-week period. These diaries were complemented with in-home visits from Pagel so he could see the moms using the product in a natural setting.

Although this quick $1,500 project worked for Bissell's situation, Pagel cautions that such

shoestring ethnography isn't for every project. Observational research can be do-it-yourself if business risk is relatively low, if it's a category that the marketer knows well, and if there are few differences across markets or regions. But marketers shouldn't "try this at home" if they're investigating a brand-new category, or require special access to a customer, say, at a store. (Wellner, 2001, p. 39)

Consumer Deprivation

Getting fresh insights about familiar products can be difficult. Often, people have a tough time expressing what something means to them because that thing is such a natural part of their lives. They take such products for granted. In these situations, you may need to force the issue a bit. One effective way to help people realize how important something is to them is to have them go without it for a period of time. In planning, this is called a *consumer deprivation* study. One of the best-known consumer deprivation studies led to the initial version of the Got Milk? campaign.

The Got Milk? campaign, designed by Goodby, Silverstein, & Partners, was the first campaign to bring about an increase in milk consumption and sales in the 1990s ("Got Milk?" 1996). The original campaign was regional in scope and had been initiated by the California Fluid Milk Processors Advisory Board. The main problem facing the board was that milk consumption had declined substantially in California during the 1980s and early 1990s, by an average of 2% to 3% each year. Reasons behind the decline were consumer concerns about milk's fat content, a feeling that milk was for kids, and milk's overall boring image in comparison with other beverages, mainly sodas. Past campaigns had attempted to stem declining milk consumption by giving milk a fun, trendy image and by running advertising that featured healthy-looking people. Though this advertising had been successful in shifting attitudes toward milk (more than 50% of Californians agreed that "I should drink more milk than I do"), these attitudes were not translating into sales. In approaching the problem, the ad agency recommended targeting frequent milk users. Targeting frequent users was based on the idea that it is easier to get people to continue doing what they would normally do than it is to get people to start doing something they haven't done before.

The insight behind the Got Milk? campaign was simple. The only time people ever think about milk is when they need it and it isn't there. How did the planners from Goodby, Silverstein, & Partners generate this insight? You guessed it: with a panel study.

Participants were recruited from focus groups. These brave volunteers were asked not to use milk for a week. They were to keep a diary of everything they ate or drank in that time. What was revealed in discussions with the panel participants about their week without milk was that certain foods they loved were absolutely impossible to eat without milk. Eating a chocolate brownie or bowl of cereal was unthinkable without milk. These milk drinkers found the experience frustrating and painful.

The advertising was based on creating cravings for those foods that are impossible to eat without milk. Executions started with one of the food items (a cookie, cereal, etc.) for which milk is the essential complement. The twist in the ads was that there was no milk available to accompany the food, so both the food and the heavenly moment were ruined. The success of the initial campaign for the California Fluid Milk Processors Advisory Board prompted the DMI, a national dairy organization, to adopt the campaign as well ("Got Milk?" 1996). At the national level, additional executions were created. In one national execution, hell was presented as an eternity with all the chocolate chip cookies you could eat but no milk.

GENERAL ISSUES WITH PANEL STUDIES

When considering a panel study, you need to ask yourself a few questions. The first question is, of course, "Is a panel study appropriate?" Panel studies seem to work best when the participants have a defined task, such as living without milk or trying a new product or service. Consumers seem capable of making observations of their own behavior, thoughts, and feelings if the task is specific. They generally seem to have a good time doing it as well.

Panel studies can also give you access to settings that would otherwise be difficult to observe. Instead of traveling with businesspeople, a panel of business travelers can give you ethnographic insights into the life of the business traveler. So if the setting you need to observe is difficult to get firsthand access to, a panel study may be appropriate. Panel studies require a literate audience that can keep records for you. Make sure your participants are capable of observing themselves and reporting those observations.

A second major question is, "What should the composition of my panel be?" That all depends on the nature of the product and your consumers. In the Got Milk? and Steam N' Clean examples, one local panel worked well for each situation because there weren't strong regional differences in product use or in the nature of consumers who would use the product. A milk drinker in California is probably similar to a milk drinker in New York. However, if there are strong regional differences in the use of your product, or if your product is used by diverse consumer segments, you will need to structure your panels accordingly.

How long should a panel study last? For most tasks, 2 or 3 weeks seem to work well. That's enough time for consumers to get accustomed to the task in their everyday lives but not long enough for them to grow tired of the exercise.

Some research companies employ longer panel studies. For example, some cable networks have a regular group of participants who watch and comment on network programming. These panels can last for one or more television seasons, so it is possible to execute longer panel studies. Longer studies may be necessary, depending on the purchase cycle of your product, seasonality, and so on. When you do longer panel studies, there are special issues to consider. First, you will likely experience member dropout. You will need to decide whether to replace a dropout or just let the group continue with fewer participants. Second, no matter how dedicated the panel member, you will have lapses in record keeping. People get busy, and your project may take on a lower priority for participants the longer the research project runs. Finally, staying with the same panel participants too long may result in "groupthink," where you lose the ability to generate fresh or unique insights. If panel members stay too long, they can also become corporate insiders and begin to lose their consumer perspective in favor of a business perspective.

Thus far in this chapter, we've talked about various research techniques that can help you generate good strategic insights. There is one essential element in all these techniques that we have to address. That is, it's useless to go to the trouble of conducting research if you aren't ready to listen. Believe it or not, listening is not as easy as you may think.

GETTING READY TO LISTEN

John Winsor, founder of Radar Communication—a Boulder, Colorado–based research firm that specializes in observation research—commented that some people have the impression that research has to be complicated, new and innovative, and expensive. But according to Winsor, those people are missing the point. He claims, "It's not about the research; it's all about listening" (Wellner, 2001, p. 39).

Research and planning require exceptional listening skills. Too many times, focusing on innovative techniques and the pressure to come up with that one great insight on which to build a profitable strategy gets in the way of hearing consumers. Also, personal experience can aid a planner in developing strategy, but it can interfere with your hearing. Learning to listen takes work. Planners and researchers must prepare themselves to listen.

Before starting to work with ethnographic research, do a little research on yourself. Have someone interview you about your thoughts and feelings regarding your target market. If no one is available to interview you, try writing down everything you think you know about this market. Who do you think these people are? What do you think their lives are like? What do you think they value? What are their greatest joys and fears? What do they like to buy? What music, TV shows, films, and so on. do you think they prefer? How do you feel about this group? Do you like them or dislike them? Do you have issues with what you perceive as their values or beliefs?

Good planning is the culmination of information and experience—all brought together by the planner. It will never be unbiased or objective. Nothing is, and that's OK. However, it is useful to understand how your preconceived notions of the target market may impact your interpretation and use of the ethnographic research results. Knowing how you feel can help you *bracket* off your preconceived notions for a time and enhance your ability to hear how your targeted consumers make sense of their world.

This task can also help your account team and creatives understand the biases and assumptions they are bringing to the project. As a planner, you not only have to prepare yourself to listen, but you have to prepare your account team, client, and creatives to listen as well.

SUMMARY

In this chapter, we've established that the overarching goal of ethnographic studies is achieving an emic understanding of our target consumers' lives and the meanings they ascribe to our products and services. Emic understandings are essential if we want to generate strategy that will break through the clutter and be meaningful to our targeted consumers.

Reaching emic understanding requires using ethnographic research techniques. Such techniques range from time-intensive exercises of living with our consumers and experiencing their daily lives firsthand to participating in specific consumer activities, such as shopping. Panel studies can give us ethnographic insights when we don't have the time or money to actively participate in various activities with our consumers.

Now that we've learned about various ethnographic methods, we turn our attention to developing the specialized skills you will need to execute a successful ethnographic study. One of the core skills needed to achieve emic understanding is interviewing. Don't be surprised if interviewing isn't as easy as it first seems. Read on to learn why and how to do it better.

KEY TERMS

accompanied shopping: A participant observation method in which the researcher goes shopping with consumers.

bracketing: Becoming aware of your preconceived notions of consumers so you can see how your assumptions may impact your ability to hear consumers.

consumer deprivation: Asking consumers to do without a familiar product in order to assess what the product really means to them.

covert: Going into a research setting without the participants knowing you're researching them. We do not recommend this strategy.

debriefing: Letting your research participants know generally what you've discovered in the research project; can serve as a validity check for your analysis.

diaries: Written and/or photographic accounts of your participants' experiences, compiled by your participants over a specified time period.

emergent design: A research design that can change and evolve over the course of a study in order to get the best possible information. This is considered a major strength of qualitative research.

emic: Analysis from within the culture.

ethnography: The study of people and the cultures they create.

etic: Analysis from outside the culture.

gaining access: Being allowed into a natural setting to conduct research, or being allowed to talk with the people you are interested in researching.

going native: Becoming a full participant in a culture; losing your perspective as a researcher.

information saturation or *data redundancy:* When you're confident that you're no longer hearing new information/perspectives from your participants.

observer effect: The fact that people often change their behavior when they know they are being observed. Time and experience can help you overcome this.

panel study: A study conducted over time with the same group of people.

participant observation: A type of study in which the researchers actually participate in the phenomenon they are studying.

rapport: Establishing a level of comfort with the people you are researching in order to get honest answers.

resonate: To connect. We want our marketing messages to resonate or connect with the culture of our participants.

snowballing: A method of recruiting additional research participants based on referrals from current participants.

validity: In qualitative research, validity means representing your participants' understandings of their world as best you can.

EXERCISES

1.   Grab a friend and go shopping! Your research question is, "How do consumers experience their 'favorite store'?" Start by asking your participant to identify his favorite store. Then go with him for a visit. Have him tell you what it feels like to be in the store. Have him show you where he usually goes first in the store. Ask him what he likes about the experience. Ask him what he would tell others about this store. Watch him interact with salespeople. Drain his brain about the store while he's in it! Then go to a place where you can sit down and talk some more. Ask him how the experience of shopping in the store you were just in compares with shopping in other stores. Ask him about behaviors you observed while you were in the store with him. Play a projective game with him by asking him a question such as, "If the store were a person, what would that person be like?" After the conversation, go home and try to convey in writing what the experience of shopping in the store was to your friend. Try to use his words as much as possible.

2.   Got a favorite product? One that's become such a part of your life that you take it for granted? Then do without it for a week. Write down every time you miss having that product. When do you miss it? What do you miss about it? What would you give to have it at that moment? How do you feel without the product? In other words, conduct a consumer deprivation study on yourself. After your weeklong experience, examine your written accounts of living without the product. How can you convey to others what it was like to be without the product? Use accounts from your diary to help you explain the experience to others.

3.   What do you know about seniors (people 65 and older)? Write down everything you think you know. Have a friend conduct an interview regarding seniors with you as the interviewee. Who

were you thinking of when you were being interviewed or when you were writing your thoughts? What in your experience has led you to your conclusions? Do you think you've accurately captured what it is like to be a senior? Why or why not? What you've just done is conduct a bracketing interview to help you explore your preconceived notions regarding a target market. Getting these ideas out and on paper can help you see how your preconceived notions may impact what you hear when actually researching your target market.

RELATED READING

Geertz, C. (1973). *The interpretation of cultures*. New York, NY: Basic Books.
Jorgensen, D. (1989). *Participant observation: A methodology for human studies*. Thousand Oaks, CA: Sage.
Lecompte, M., & Schensul, J. (1999). *Designing and conducting ethnographic research*. New York, NY: Rowman & Littlefield.

4

Listening to Consumers

THE QUALITATIVE INTERVIEW

Interviewing has become common practice in American life. Reporters interview sources to gather information for their stories. Sports broadcasters interview athletes about how it feels to have just won or lost the big game. Police officers interview suspects to gather information about who may have committed the crime. Human resource workers interview prospective employees. Media talk show hosts interview almost anyone who has a 60-second story to tell, and when no one is left to interview, they interview each other about how well their talk shows are going. Furthermore, the development of software for video conferencing over the Internet has streamlined the process for conducting such interviews at a distance.

Unfortunately, none of these well-known interview types has much in common with what we call the *qualitative interview*. The interview situations listed above are all conducted from the perspective of the person conducting the interview. A newspaper reporter comes across a juicy quote from one source and suddenly needs an opposing quote to give balance to the news story. A broadcast reporter, knowing that she will be allocated only a few seconds of airtime for her story, looks for the "sound bite" that will attract attention. The police officer seeks to confirm or destroy the suspect's alibi. In each of these interview situations, the interview itself lasts only a short time and the person conducting the interview has a story or structure he or she is trying to confirm. Qualitative interviewing, on the other hand, is conducted from the perspective of the person being interviewed.

CHARACTERISTICS OF QUALITATIVE INTERVIEWING

Interviewing offers the opportunity to delve deeply into the everyday worlds of meaning constructed by participants. Through interviewing, the planner can discover complex social connections and gain insight into the cultural nuances of the participants' worlds. Interviewing is totally dependent on gaining access to and cooperation from a small set of participants and on the participants talking honestly and truthfully with the researcher. Except for highly sensitive product purchases, access to and cooperation from consumers is not usually a barrier. Most people like to talk about their lives, even to strangers. However, the data from qualitative interviews are only as good as the researcher's interviewing skills and her ability to interpret data, both of which are best learned through experience. Qualitative interviews should be conducted in natural settings for an extended duration and from the participant's point of view.

Not all qualitative interviews are with consumers. When the makers of Tylenol wanted to reposition the brand, ad agency planners first spent hours interviewing the people who make it—researchers, scientists, doctors, and executives—before interviewing consumers. The agency for UPS first conducted interviews with UPS management and department heads before moving outside the company to conduct interviews with the potential users of UPS—shipping managers, mid-level managers, and senior-level decision makers.

Natural Settings

A qualitative interview is a face-to-face interaction between a researcher and a participant, usually conducted in the location where the behavior of interest occurs. In all qualitative research, *natural settings* are preferred over artificial ones. A natural setting could be in a tavern or bar, at a grocery store, in an airplane, on a playing field, or standing in the middle of a stream in the Great Smoky Mountains National Park. Qualitative researchers believe in going where their research participants are rather than bringing the research participants into the researcher's domain. The emphasis on interviewing in a natural setting comes from the qualitative research belief that context is important in determining meaning. Conducting qualitative research means getting people to talk about what specific things mean to them, and this is more easily accomplished in the natural setting.

Consider, for example, that you wanted to know the meaning of pickup trucks to their owners. You could invite truck owners into the corporate research offices to talk about their trucks, or you could go to the homes of the truck owners, ride in their trucks with them, and generally get them to talk about their trucks. Sitting in the truck with the owner suggests many contextual cues about ownership that are lacking in a conference room interview. You might observe a number of features about truck ownership that would otherwise escape you. For example, where is the truck parked overnight? Is it left outside while the family car gets the benefit of the garage? Or is the truck parked in the garage? What kind of accessories and items are inside the truck? Is there a gun rack? Are items dangling from the rearview mirror? Is the truck interior clean or dirty? Who drives the truck (only the owner?) and for what kinds of trips? Who in the family has a personal set of keys to the truck? Observing and asking these types of questions will lead to a deeper, richer interpretation of the meaning of truck ownership.

Of Long Duration

A good qualitative interview will usually last from 30 minutes to 2 hours. The exact number of minutes is less important than the fact that the planner gives the participant sufficient opportunity to say all that he can about the item of interest and, equally important, that the researcher has sufficient opportunity to hear all that the participant has to say. Obviously, some participants are more verbose than others; some elaborate greatly on their answers, and others pretty much stick to short, dry answers. Often, you'll find that as the interview continues, the participant opens up and is willing to talk more freely. Most people enjoy talking about themselves, their work, their hobbies, their families, and their possessions. If participants have been told in advance about the topic of the interview, though not necessarily the planner's specific interest, they will talk more freely.

From the Participant's Point of View

The goal of most qualitative research is to come to understand the participant's world in the way the participant does and in the concepts the participant uses. This is a rather noble and lofty goal—one that's almost impossible to achieve. Nevertheless, it suggests that researchers will not impose a world of meaning (and words) on the participant's world but will instead seek to understand the meaning things have in the world of the participant. Often, the researcher will have to assume a naive and uninformed position to really listen to what people are saying.

A common mistake made by beginning qualitative interviewers is to add too much of their own commentary to the interview, thus negating their opportunity to really hear what the participant is saying. Qualitative interviewing is extremely demanding intellectual work. It requires the ability to maintain a single focus of thought for several hours while formulating probes and follow-up questions at the same time. Understanding things from the other person's perspective, or from the insider's perspective, suggests that the interviewer will do very little talking, will refrain from imposing concepts or judgments on what the participant is saying, and will gently lead the participant through the areas of discussion.

GETTING READY TO INTERVIEW

Preparing the Interview Guide

In getting ready to conduct a series of qualitative interviews, the planner should prepare a discussion guideline of broad topics, moving from the general to the specific. Usually four or five topics or questions are all that can be covered in a single interview. The first question should always be broad and invite the participant to talk about his life, his work, or his family. In a qualitative world, everything is connected to everything else, and one of your goals as a qualitative researcher should be to uncover those connections. Possessions, brands, buying habits, and choices of where to shop and what to buy are not isolated decisions; they're all connected to other aspects of participants' lives.

If you start the interview with a direct question related to a narrow focus, you'll never uncover these connections. The list of four or five questions will serve as a guide to what you want to hear about, and you'll create most of the direct questions as the interview progresses. Qualitative interviewing asks participants to talk about things they have experienced, so asking participants to conjecture and speculate on things they have not experienced is not likely to yield reliable information.

An *interview guide* for cat owners, for example, that seeks to understand not only the meaning of the cat to its owner but also why cat owners buy certain brands of cat box filler or cat food or cat treats might consist of the following broad topics:

1. *Family.* Tell me about your family (e.g., spouse, children, grandchildren) and neighborhood (e.g., type of housing, neighborhood, neighbors).

2. *Pets.* Tell me about your family's pets (e.g., dogs, birds, fish, snakes, rabbits, cats).

3. *Cats.* Tell me about the cats you have (prompts: cats' names, personalities, types, behavior, care, feeding, where sheltered, toys, whether neutered or spayed, major caregiver).

4. *Cat foods, cat treats, cat care.* If the owner has not introduced the topic of interest to the researcher, then the researcher might ask more specifically at this point such questions as, Do you buy cat box filler for your cat? Where is the cat box kept? How often is it changed? Who usually changes it? Who buys the cat box filler? Where do you buy it? What brand do you buy? Have you tried different brands?

Note that the interview guide moves from general questions to specific questions. By going in this order, the researcher hopes to uncover meaningful connections to buying behavior. Does the fact that the neighbor has a fierce dog, for example, lead to certain types of cat confinement that might not occur otherwise? Does the owner feel guilty about leaving the cat alone and, therefore, compensate by buying more expensive brands for the cat? These are the kinds of connections that can be discovered only through qualitative research.

Preparing the Data Sheet

You should have a *data sheet* for each participant you interview. On it, you should record the participant's name, address, and any other information pertinent to the reason for your study, such as marital status, family size, household type, income, type of job, and certain kinds of possessions. You won't be able to think of all possible relevant variables to record, but make a note of those that seem important before you begin the study. Others may arise during the course of the interview, or it may take two or three interviews before you see a connection between what you're interested in and some unforeseen item. For example, it may not be just that a participant is married but, also, how long the person has been married that explains certain kinds of behavior.

In addition to a data sheet, most qualitative research will require that you gain the participants' informed consent, evidenced by their signatures on consent forms. Such forms usually address a variety of things, including the nature of the research to be conducted, whether the participants are to be paid, what use will be made of the data (usually with the stipulation that none of the participants' names will be attached to the data), any potential harm that may come to the participants, and a clause stating the participants' right to withdraw from the study at their own choosing.

Preparing the Mechanics

Most qualitative interviewers record their interviews with a hand-held tape or digital recorder. Condenser microphones can be unreliable, so arrange to have a good-quality external microphone attached to the recorder and always check the volume and make a sample recording in the exact place where you will conduct the interview.

For example, if you're interviewing a participant at her kitchen table, you can make small talk with the participant while you set up the recorder. Place the recorder between the two of you, but make sure it's set to one side so it doesn't interfere with the direct line of sight between you and the participant. Turn on the recorder and in a normal tone of voice, say the date and where you are and the type of interview. Then replay it to make sure you're getting a good-quality recording. If you don't—and you later discover that you have left the volume too low or have left the pause button on, or have forgotten to put a tape in—you will have lost not only a half-day's work but much valuable information! So always take a minute or so to check the quality of the recording you're getting. Be sure that the microphone is not too close to an air-conditioning unit, for example, or the background noise may obliterate all the conversation.

CONDUCTING THE INTERVIEW

For most researchers, the first qualitative interview is a bit disappointing. Many who are accustomed to using a structured interview guide have never really learned to listen to what the participant says. Rather, they're only half listening while thinking of what they are going to say next. As a general rule in qualitative interviewing, what you ask next is always based on what the participant has just said. When you do this, you allow the participant to make and reveal the connections of things rather than imposing your connections on the participants' words. Once you've completed the data sheet and have asked the participant to talk about himself or herself generally, move to the area of interest to you by introducing the topic at one level of abstraction above your item of interest. For instance, if you want to know about truck ownership, start at the level of vehicle ownership or how one gets to and from work rather than posing a pointed question about trucks. Let's say that a participant says,

> In this house, there's me and my wife. And we have a daughter who's in third grade. She's 8 years old and will be 9 next June. I work at a window replacement company, and my wife's a bookkeeper for an insurance company. We got two dogs and one cat.

Your next question should be related to what the participant just said and should move toward your topic of interest. If your subject is dog food, then you might say, "Tell me about your pets." If the subject is job satisfaction, then you might say, "Tell me about your job." If the subject is marital relationships, you might say, "Tell me about your wife." If the subject is trucks, you might say, "How do you and your wife get to work?" Notice that almost any topic can be pulled from this brief self-description, but the appropriate one is the topic that moves in the direction of the interview subject and is still one level of abstraction above that focus. First, ask the respondent to talk about the dogs, waiting to see if he introduces the topic of dog food. If he does, you can be fairly sure that he'll reveal how the subject "feeding the dog" or "dog food" is related in his mind to the concept of "dogs."

Regardless of what the participant mentions, some things you absolutely do not want to say are, "I have a dog, too," "My sister worked for an insurance company once," or "I have a daughter." Although rules of polite conversation might suggest that you contribute to the conversation, a qualitative interview is not a two-sided conversation. You're not conducting the interview so the participant can learn about you; rather, you're conducting it so you can learn about the participant. Avoid all attempts to interject facts about yourself into the conversation, as they will just detract from your concentrating on what the participant is saying.

Though most of the situations qualitative interviewers encounter while developing advertising strategy are rather benign and nonthreatening, think about occasions when you might call on your interviewing skills in the name of developing self-help programs or community programs. In those cases, you often want to be absolutely sure that you do nothing to indicate approval of the behavior. Consider this revelation from a woman who physically abused her husband and was ordered to a treatment program: "It's his fault anyway because he ain't much of a man. If he was a real man, he wouldn't have let me hit him with the iron skillet." Here, you've discovered a rather strange, but nonetheless common, belief among husband abusers: "It's his fault." You'd want to refrain from saying or doing anything that reinforced this belief, such as, "Yeah, I would have hit him, too" or "He surely deserved to be hit." In the same way, refrain from approving of the consumption behavior that participants talk about. Your goal is to understand the behavior from the participant's perspective, not to add your perspective to it. Similarly, consider this revelation from an unmarried, pregnant teenager: "For breakfast, I had a bottle of pop and some pig skins." Unless you're providing nutritional advice—and no matter how much you want to chastise the participant for her diet and its possible effects on her unborn baby—you must refrain from making judgments. Approve, and you seemingly condone the behavior. Disapprove, and you greatly diminish the chances that the participant will continue to answer openly. Be content to take the role of recorder while you're gathering the information.

As you move from point to point in the qualitative interview, try to pose your questions and prompts in terms of and in relation to what the participant has just said. Avoid asking participants to speculate with "if" and "what if" questions. Rather, ask them to recall a time in their lives when something did occur. If you want to know if dog owners take their sick animals to veterinarians, it's better to ask, "Has your dog ever been sick?" and proceed from there than it is to ask, "If your dog were sick, would you take it to the veterinarian?" Though the difference in wording is slight, the difference in accuracy may be great. One question asks the participant to tell about something that has happened, and the other asks the participant to speculate about something he might do if something did happen. Keep your questions grounded in the real and the concrete.

At some point, the participant may have revealed all that he can about a particular aspect of the subject or the subject itself. At that point, it can be useful to summarize your discussion thus far and ask if anything else occurs to the participant. You might say, for example, "We've talked about your family car and truck, that you drive the truck to and from work, that you use the truck to haul trash and recyclables to the recycling center, that you don't have shelter for the truck but wish you did, that you use the truck when you buy gardening materials and building supplies, that the truck is 'yours' and the car is 'hers' but that you take care of the maintenance on both of them, and that you drive the car and not the truck to church on Sundays." Then you might ask, "Are there any other places or times when you drive the car but not the truck or drive the truck but not the car?" Your participant might recall that when it's snowing, he drives his wife to work in the truck for safety. Now you have another line of discussion, one dealing with truck safety; once that's exhausted, you can return to prompts regarding appropriate places to drive the truck.

You'll notice that qualitative interviewing does not always proceed in a linear fashion, nor should it. Though you have your list of four or five topic areas to cover, how you get to them is less important than the fact that you do get to them using the concepts and meanings your participants use.

Sometimes, a participant will use a word or phrase that seems to have a special or insider meaning to her. In these cases, it is best not to assume that the word means what you think it means but, rather, to ask the participant to explain it.

For example, a participant, in talking about her husband's trips to the grocery store, revealed, "When I'm not with him, he goes down the potato chip and ice cream aisle." Few, if any, grocery stores stock potato chips and ice cream in the same aisle. So, rather than assuming we understand the participant, it's better to say, "I'm not sure I understand. Can you tell me what a potato chip and ice cream aisle is?" In this case, it was any aisle that stocked junk food—but junk food that the wife didn't approve of the husband buying. Words and phrases that have unique meanings to the participants but are rarely found in a dictionary are called *emic* words. Listen carefully for emic words; they can reveal how participants construct their everyday worlds.

INTRODUCING OBJECTS

Sometimes, you will have an object such as a proposed advertisement, a logo, a prototype of a new product, a set of statements, or a description of something you want the participant to respond to. These items are best introduced at the end of the interview, instead of at the beginning or in the middle, because they have great power to stunt and skew discussion. If you show participants a proposed advertisement at the beginning of the interview, chances are it will color and direct most of what they say. It's better to listen to what the participants have to say and introduce the commercial at the end. Otherwise, participants may decide you are interested only in their opinion of the object. Placing an object at the end gives both the participant and the researcher a rich base from which to evaluate it.

In a study about how adult learners decide to return to school, we interviewed adult learners in depth about the decision-making process, when they decided to return to school, who had been influential in their decision, and how long they labored over the decision. At the end of the interview, participants were asked to judge, in their own terms and words, the value of a commercial encouraging adult learners to enroll at a particular school. By the time the commercial was shown, that the commercial badly missed the mark was quite obvious in each case. The planners not only knew that the commercial missed the mark but also had gathered considerable insight as to why.

ENDING THE INTERVIEW

When you have properly summarized, in various steps along the way, all that the participant has told you and the participant has nothing else to say, then it's time to close the interview. Turn off the tape recorder. Thank the participant for her time, and make arrangements for the participant to contact you in case she thinks of something else she wants to tell you. Indicate how helpful the participant has been to your research project and ask if she has any questions. Also, ask for permission to follow up with the participant if needed. At this point, look carefully for any clues from the participant that she may have more to say. For some participants, turning off the tape recorder and signaling an end to the interview brings on a greater openness to reveal. This is more likely to be true when you're interviewing about personally sensitive topics, so don't rush away from the interview too quickly.

ANALYZING THE TRANSCRIPTS

Analyzing qualitative data actually begins at the time of data collection. Listening carefully to what your participant says and posing your next question based on what has just been said is an early form of analysis. You begin to see how concepts are related in the participant's world. Likewise, you should perform at least a cursory analysis of each interview before you proceed to the next one.

Conducting a qualitative interview demands so much concentrated attention that two or three interviews per day is all you should attempt to do. If you're interviewing in a language that is not your native language, be satisfied to do only two interviews per day at most. Otherwise, you'll become so mentally tired that you will miss important details during subsequent interviews.

Your initial analysis might consist of a brief written summary of the interview along with a series of questions that point out potential connections. Particularly when you're working with other qualitative interviewers, writing memos to yourself and to your research team members is important. Keep in mind that you're trying to discover things that are true for the group of individuals being interviewed, not idiosyncratic, meaning for one individual alone. If you have in your mind even a sketchy analysis of your first interview, you'll be able to see some similarities in the second interview as you conduct it.

Even though you may write a summary of each interview, preparing a full *transcript* of each interview is still important. The planner, or else a clerical assistant, can do this. In either case, checking the accuracy of the transcription against the recorded tape is important. An advantage of completing the transcription yourself is that it gives you another opportunity to hear the interview and perform some analysis along the way. It also gives you a chance to critique yourself as an interviewer, asking whether you posed appropriate prompts and if you followed all the important lines of questioning. Usually, the less talking you do and the more talking the participant does, the better the quality of your interview will be. Do a quick line count of the interview. If you were speaking half the time, you've probably contributed too much. As a rule of thumb, a good interview has the participant talking 80% or more of the time. As you become more skilled at interviewing, you'll note that you talk less and listen more.

When do you know you have interviewed a sufficient number of people? This is obviously related to your research purpose and the size of the overall group. However, a point of *redundancy* usually sets in between the 8th and the 15th interview; that is, when an additional interview reveals no new information, it is time to stop interviewing. Obviously, additional interviews would give you additional examples of the phenomenon you're studying, but understanding the essence of the research topic is what's most important to you, not collecting as many examples of it as you can.

After you have completed and transcribed the interviews, the really difficult intellectual work begins. Analyzing qualitative transcripts requires an open and creative mind. It requires reading and rereading the transcripts and fully immersing yourself in the text. A helpful starting point is to read through all the transcripts and summaries first and make notes of what relationships seem to exist. If you're studying a process—for example, buying a car—then try to fit things into a timeline and ask yourself how the participants' activities changed from recognizing the need to buy a car to the actual purchase.

Developing a Coding Scheme

Qualitative researchers view the human world as one of purposeful activity. Individuals encounter objects, situations, and events in their lives. They interpret the meaning of such things and then plan courses of action that fit that interpretation. Individuals are not passive beings acted upon by the world but, rather, active individuals going about their daily lives. For this reason, when developing a *coding scheme*, try to code your transcripts by activities, such as interpretations, actions, strategies, and the conditions under which these occur. Rather than using passive codes such as "happy" or "sad," make the codes active: "experiencing joy" or "regretting past actions." Seeing individuals as active beings will help you find the connections between their acts—and also the conditions under which these acts occur and their consequences. Consider that many people, when they are feeling blue, will buy a little reward to make themselves feel better. We can construct this line of behavior as follows: experiencing disappointment leads to feeling sad, which leads to buying a product or service, which leads to experiencing upbeat emotions. This is an almost universal buying phenomenon. Some people will buy CDs, others might buy a magazine, a book, perfume, clothing, or treat themselves to a manicure. It is not the physical qualities of the CDs, magazines, books, perfumes, clothing, or manicures that group these products together but, rather, the meaning of each product to the individual who purchases it. In a qualitative world, everything is connected to everything else.

Analyzing qualitative data requires you to ask a series of questions about each piece of data you collect. One question that is always useful is, "What is this an example of?" Qualitative analysis begins inductively. The researcher finds an example of something and then tries to match it conceptually to something else. The researcher proceeds in this fashion, adding things, changing the definitions of things, creating new categories, and looking for how categories are connected until he has exhausted all the data.

Consider the following quote from a series of interviews about husband and wife shopping behavior. The wife is talking about how her husband influences her buying behavior.

Wife: Occasionally, there will be things that I don't purchase because my husband may feel it's too extravagant. I don't feel it's too extravagant, but he might.

Interviewer: Can you give me an example?

Wife: You're going to laugh! I like (named specialty store) when I am in the mall. I may want to get their antibacterial soap that may cost 10 dollars when we could go to (named discount store) and get the equivalent for maybe a dollar. And if he is with me, I will not buy things like that. It would just drive him crazy until we left the store or until we got home. That kind of thing definitely stands out, but you know if I come back and I'm alone and there is something I want, you better believe I'll do it. I won't take it home and hide it, but it's just easier not to have to deal with "I can't believe you're buying that."

At the surface level, this quote could be considered an example of buying soap. At another level, however, it's an example of strategies women use to buy what they want. And this particular strategy consists of the activities of (a) delaying the purchase, (b) returning to the store alone, and (c) buying the product. For other participants, this strategy extended to (d) hiding the purchase at home and (e) having it magically appear at a later date. The objects varied across interviews, but the strategies were much the same.

Consider the following portion of the same transcript. The wife is talking about buying clothes.

> Our tastes are different. If I ask him what he thinks, and he agrees, then that's good. But if we disagree, then I get what I want anyway.

The exchange is about buying clothes, of course, but at another level of analysis, it could be labeled "preferencing judgment," because the participant gives greater value to her own judgment than to her husband's. Now we have two strategies that suggest how women get their way: (a) shopping alone and (b) preferencing judgment.

In subsequent interviews, we would look for additional examples of these two strategies and for additional strategies as well. In developing our list of strategies, it's not necessary that each participant reveal or engage in each one. We're only trying to identify and understand the use of such strategies, not make a claim about the distribution of the strategies among the participants.

Knowing that shoppers use such strategies provides insight into developing a creative theme and constructing the visuals for messages. In our example of women's shopping strategies, the women likely need confirmation that they're doing the right thing. Constructing messages that implicitly condone the shopping strategies revealed in the interviews, reinforce the correctness of independent female shopper judgment, and express the value of self-reward allow the advertiser to fit the message within the reality constructed by the shopper. Given that the strategies really are little games that wives play with their husbands, a light-hearted tone would also seem appropriate.

Qualitative data analysis is nonlinear and sometimes quite messy. Researchers are great doodlers, writing down concepts, drawing lines of relationship from one concept to another, listing conditions under which things occur, and marking up transcripts with questions and observations. It's all part of the job of analysis. Don't be concerned if you can't immediately find all the relationships in your data. They have a way of hiding from you and then all of a sudden popping out. Gaining insight is a creative process over which the planner does not have total control. It may take a dozen iterations before anything or everything begins to make sense.

Of course, account planners do sometimes collect their data via telephone or Internet, but these are generally poor substitutes for face-to-face interviews. Interviewers have to establish trust with their participants, and in addition to reducing the contextual clues available to the researcher, technology reduces the number of contextual clues available to participants, which slows the development of trust. A relaxed attitude, a show of genuine interest in the participant and what she has to say, and a high level of attentiveness help develop trust during the course of the interview. When these are not visible, trust builds more slowly.

INTERVIEWING GROUPS

Rather than interviewing individuals one at a time, interviewing groups of individuals can be more economical and faster and can produce data from participant interaction that would not be available otherwise.

Advertising research has a history of convening groups of individuals in rooms with two-way mirrors and videotaping capabilities and then asking a series of questions related to an advertising problem. This technique—focus groups—has been much abused because it has primarily sought confirmation of researchers' ideas and concepts rather than seeking meaning from the insider's perspective. Most of all, it violates the qualitative tenet of going to the participants and conducting the research in a natural setting.

However, *group interviewing* may be quite appropriate when (a) we can judge without doubt that the topic of interest is of considerable importance to the participants selected, (b) we want to add to or confirm what we've discovered through other research methods, and (c) the behavior we want to understand occurs naturally in a group setting. Certain events in participants' lives carry great importance. These might include, for example, choosing a college, getting married, having children, getting divorced, suffering a life-threatening disease, or buying a home. Gathering diverse individuals into a single group to discuss these experiences would be more economical than interviewing each person individually. If you're forming a group of consumers based on brand purchase, then selecting brand loyalists or heavy users of the product is better if you want to gather meaningful data that can provide insight into buying patterns. Qualitative interviewing deals with the things of importance in the everyday lives of individuals. But just because something is of great importance to the planner doesn't mean it's of equal importance to the participants.

New mothers are concerned about what they feed their babies, and such concern obviously may lead to choosing one brand of baby food over another. The new-motherhood status binds the group, not reliance on a particular brand, and the insight you seek is the connection between motherhood and brand choice, not just brand usage.

Sometimes, a researcher will conduct individual interviews with consumers to develop initial insight and then add more economical discussion groups consisting of the same or similar people. If the situation warrants it, that's fine, but you need to be aware that the order in which you use research methods can affect the results of your study. Because of the social sensitivity of some behaviors and purchases, it is better to conduct the personal interviews first and follow them with focus groups. A person may express a socially correct opinion in a group and then feel compelled to maintain that opinion during an individual interview as well. If you're in doubt about which method to use first, choose individual interviewing before conducting group interviews.

After completing 10 to 12 individual interviews, you may wonder if your initial interpretations of the data are valid. At this point, planners will sometimes ask the individuals who have been interviewed to convene as a group to evaluate the research results. Such a group meeting not only has the advantage of helping with the data analysis but also provides additional data and insight as group members interact with one another.

Sometimes, the behavior you primarily want to understand is group behavior. Keeping in mind the importance of contextual meaning in qualitative research, adherence to its theoretical foundation suggests that studying the behavior in the group setting is appropriate. Consider, as an example, this question: "What do school children eat for lunch?" We could ask the parent who prepares the lunch, but the parent cannot answer the question. He knows only what is prepared and packed for the child's lunch. We could even take an inventory of lunch bags as children enter the school or the cafeteria at lunch. But, again, this would tell us only what has been prepared, not what is actually being eaten for lunch. Obviously, sitting at the table in the natural surroundings of the lunchroom, observing and interacting with the children, is more likely to provide a reliable answer. There, we might encounter the trading of lunch items that often occurs and observe what children are actually eating.

Families constitute another important form of group behavior. Within a family, each individual member will have a different interpretation about how the family functions and where decision making occurs. For example, individually interviewing spouses in long-lasting marriages about threats to their marriage over the years will produce some similar interpretations between spouses. Yet, for one spouse, what was regarded as a tough time may not have been experienced similarly by the other. When you interview the spouses together, you discover a slightly different shared interpretation of the marriage. Is one more accurate than the other? Of course not. In a qualitative world, multiple meanings are associated with events and all are equally true. One is not privileged over the other.

If you interview families about certain day-to-day activities, such as renting DVDs for the family to watch, selecting where to dine out, or deciding where to go on vacation, you'll discover individual truths as well as a family truth. The same would be true if you were to interview members of work groups. There are individual interpretations as well as a shared, social interpretation. Whether one is more or less applicable than another depends on why you're conducting the research. If your aim is to influence family choice of a vacation destination, then you need to understand the family decision-making process (if, in fact, there is one) and the role each family member plays in it. Is Dad relegated to paying the bills and approving the final choice, while Mom and the kids surf the World Wide Web and read brochures to develop the list of places to choose from? Or does Dad or Mom present a list of reasonable choices and other family members choose the final destination? A simple question posed to the family, such as, "Tell me how you decided as a family where you last went on vacation," can produce several extended narratives, with family members correcting and contradicting one another. Whether to conduct individual or family interviews in this case would depend on your ability to identify the major decision maker, if there is one. Even at that, you might find that other family members exert a powerful influence on the decision maker.

WHEN YOU CAN'T GAIN ACCESS TO THE NATURAL SETTING

Interviewing is considered one of the primary data collection methods in qualitative research. Sometimes, however, participants are reluctant to give you access to their homes, families, or workplaces. In these situations—and sometimes for reasons of economy—the planner might be restricted to conducting the interview by telephone or e-mail correspondence. In such interviews, you may lose much contextual information about the person or about decision making.

If you wanted to interview company presidents, for example, they might be unwilling to grant you a face-to-face interview of unspecified length. In such cases, you can agree to a specified length of, say, 20 minutes, hoping that once the interview is under way, the participant may choose to extend the time. We have seen this occur from time to time, because even busy corporate executives enjoy talking about their lives and work when they have the undivided, interested attention of a planner.

When the participants you want to interview are widely scattered geographically and your research budget is small, you may choose to interview by telephone, recognizing that you will lose contextual information. In such cases, it's best to arrange in advance a time and date for the telephone call. You can proceed much as you would in a face-to-face interview, but know that you'll be totally dependent on sound and tone of voice to help guide you. As you would in other interview situations, you can easily record the telephone interview and produce a transcript for analysis.

Two other ways to gather interview-like qualitative data are by traditional mail survey and by e-mail. With these techniques, much more responsibility and labor are placed on the participant, and the opportunities for the spontaneous prompt and requests for clarification are almost nil. However, as long as you allow participants to respond to your questions from their own perspectives and in their own words, you should be able to gain insight, though limited, into their worlds of meaning.

CLARIFYING THE SOCIAL ROLE OF QUALITATIVE INTERVIEWER

Unfortunately, no generally recognized role called "qualitative interviewer" exists in society. If someone asks you to fill out a survey in person or respond to a set of questions over the phone or via e-mail, you have a reasonably good idea of what will be involved because you understand the role of "survey taker." When you ask someone to talk to you for an hour or so about a topic of interest, your role could easily be confused with the role of spy, therapist, counselor, or confidante. Qualitative researchers are none of these, and you should be careful not to confuse the work of a qualitative researcher with the work of other occupational groups. Most qualitative researchers are not trained in counseling or advice giving of any type and should avoid doing so. However, if you have established a trusting relationship with your participant, he or she may look to you for advice. The best you can do may be to refer the participant to a resource that can offer the kind of help he or she seeks.

In addition, you should assume that most things a participant tells you are to be held in strictest confidence and not shared with anyone outside the research team. If a trusting relationship has been established, then participants may tell you things that could be damaging to them. While legal protection allows lawyers and priests to maintain client confidentiality, qualitative researchers do not have such protection. If you are ever summoned to court to testify about information revealed to you in an interview, you have no right to withhold that information unless it would also incriminate you. Fortunately, most of the work conducted by qualitative researchers isn't quite so serious, but do recognize that some people may think you are engaged in industrial espionage, corporate spying, or other unsavory activities. Telling others that you conduct qualitative interviews isn't understood nearly as easily as telling them you conduct telephone surveys. However, you should never misrepresent your purpose in order to gain access to a research site. It's acceptable to tell participants that you would like to talk with them about "things they buy," "vacation planning," "voting," or "OTC drugs" without revealing all the specifics of your study, but you should never intentionally misrepresent your purpose.

SUMMARY

Qualitative interviewing is an intellectually demanding, time-consuming process. Its goal, like that of all qualitative research, is to come to understand the meaningful world of participants as they understand it themselves.

Conducting good qualitative interviews takes time, patience, and practice; interview skills develop over time. Qualitative interviews can be conducted with individuals, with groups of individuals, in naturally occurring groups, or in a combination of these. Identifying relationships in qualitative data is a creative process over which the researcher does not have total control.

Qualitative interviews should be conducted in natural settings using an interview guide of no more than four or five topics. Discussion should move from the general to the specific and should always begin at least one level of abstraction above the researcher's topic of interest. Qualitative interviews may last from 30 minutes to 2 hours, depending on interviewer skill and the interest level of the participant.

Qualitative interviewing assumes that participants are able to describe the worlds they live in and that they're willing to do so.

Some researchers believe that some information may be below the threshold of consciousness, and even if willing, participants are unable to access it directly. Others believe that some information is so sensitive that participants are unwilling to talk about it. In these situations, planners may turn to projective techniques to help them understand the participants' worlds of meaning. The following chapter discusses the use of these techniques. Are you a donkey or a lion? Read on to find out.

KEY TERMS

coding scheme: A set of categories into which most of what participants say can be assigned.

data sheet: A sheet of paper for recording relevant demographic data about each participant in the study.

emic: From the participant's perspective, using the participant's own words.

group interview: Interviewing several individuals at the same time about the same topic. Group interviews allow for interaction among participants.

interview guide: A list of four or five topics to be covered in an interview.

natural setting: Any location where the behavior to be studied occurs naturally.

redundancy: A point in interviewing at which no new information is being revealed.

transcript: A written, verbatim record of an interview.

EXERCISES

1.   Resonance message strategies present emotions and memories that have counterparts in the experiences of a group of people. For your generation, what would be some typical resonating

experiences and emotions? How do these differ from the experiences and emotions of your parents' generation?

2.   In 21st-century America, giving your child the same name as that of your sister's child would be considered an insult. We're much too individualistic for that. But this has not always been the case. Naming of children follows different patterns in different cultures. See if you can gain insight into the naming pattern followed here: William is Henry's older brother. William marries Elizabeth, and Henry marries Mary. Henry and Mary name their first male child William. Shortly thereafter, William and Elizabeth have their first child, a male, and name him William. Then William and Elizabeth have a second son, whom they also name William. Henry and Mary have a second son, whom they name Henry. What is the name of William and Henry's father? Given this practice, you can appreciate the need for nicknames such as "Tall William," "Big William," and "Short William."

3.   Here is a partial transcript of an interview with a teenage girl who is describing her clothing purchases. What emic words can you identify?

> I needed a new dress to go to New York, so my mom and I went to the mall to look for one. I found this really awesome cocktail dress. It was low-cut and kind of short and really fierce. My mom said it made me look slutty, so I didn't buy it. But I really wanted that blue dress. Instead, I bought a turquoise one. It's all right, but it's not the one I wanted. But I don't want to go around looking like a skeeze either.

4.   You are conducting long interviews with middle school English teachers regarding job satisfaction. One teacher dislikes her job so much that she reveals she is leaving at the end of the year to accept a position as a buyer for a department store. The school principal, who has helped you gain access to the teachers, asks you if anyone has mentioned plans to leave the school. How do you respond?

5.   See Appendix 1 for a long interview assignment, an annotated transcript, and a sample page from a qualitative report.

RELATED READING

McCracken, G. (1988). *The long interview.* Newbury Park, CA: Sage.

Miles, M. B., & Huberman, A. M. (1994). *Qualitative data analysis: An expanded sourcebook* (2nd ed.). Thousand Oaks, CA: Sage.

Morgan, D. (1988). *Focus groups as qualitative research.* Newbury Park, CA: Sage.

5

Projective and Elicitation Techniques

What would your response be if you found out that customers for an account you're working on described your client as a donkey but the employees who worked at the company described themselves as racehorses, jaguars, or lions? What kinds of conclusions could you draw from these data? Well, you might reach the same conclusion as NOP Research Group (2001), the market research agency that conducted this study for an office equipment manufacturer. The client ordered this research after suspecting that its customers did not feel the same way about the company as did the employees who worked there. To figure out whether the client was correct, NOP conducted in-depth interviews with customers. Included in the interviews was the question, "If this company was an animal, what animal would it be?" Analysis of the data suggested that the company's employees and customers held vastly different perceptions of it—donkeys and lions being quite different, after all. The results of this research helped determine that an image problem existed; the client subsequently took steps to correct the image problem and improve business practices.

It is possible to uncover what people think and feel by asking them a direct question in the context of an interview, but that doesn't always work. In the typical interview, participants don't always feel comfortable sharing their innermost feelings with a stranger, and that's often what the researcher is. Furthermore, consumers sometimes aren't sure why they buy a product or choose one brand over another because the reason is buried deep in their subconsciousness. And even if they do know why they buy, consumers don't want to appear irrational or stupid. They want to appear normal and will sometimes give you socially acceptable answers. Or they'll avoid telling you exactly what they think just to be polite. In short, a lot of times, people—for a variety of reasons—just aren't straight up with interviewers.

In these instances, the inability to get at a consumer's real feelings can be a problem. Let's use two national brands of toilet paper as an example: Charmin and Angel Soft. In some instances, a consumer might choose Angel Soft simply because she likes the picture of an angel on the packaging. To her, angels are soft and gentle, and she sees them as keeping watch over her children. In fact, she used angels as part of the decorating motif in her baby's room. Angels also align with her religious beliefs. But she thinks these explanations sound frivolous and aren't exactly good reasons to buy a brand, so she might tell an interviewer that she purchases Angel Soft over Charmin because it's cheaper/softer/her husband likes it and so on. All these sound like perfectly good reasons to buy a brand, and the interviewer will probably accept them at face value. But they aren't the real reasons she buys Angel Soft. The influence of the product packaging—the association of angels with the brand—is important for an interviewer to know, but direct questioning won't uncover it.

Let's try a few more scenarios. Let's say that you were interviewing the same consumer and showed her different characters associated with toilet paper, asking her what each meant: Mr. Whipple, angels, pastel flowers, clouds, horses, puppies—all those visuals you associate with toilet paper and a couple you don't (just so she wouldn't guess what your real intentions were). Using a visual stimulus, she might be more prone to fess up to the meaning of angels in her life. The visual stimulus might also open the floodgates to information leading to insights about the influence of packaging on her purchase decisions. Or you might ask her to construct a story about the two brands of toilet paper. Her story about Charmin might involve the character Mr. Whipple and how he resembles her grandfather, the person she trusts most in her life. Her story about Angel Soft might very well focus on the angel associations the brand holds for her (e.g., "In heaven, the only brand of toilet paper in the bathrooms is Angel Soft"). Both these techniques would allow the researcher "access" to the real reason why she buys Angel Soft: because of the angels.

The approach that helped in the above example is called a projective technique. *Projective techniques* involve the use of stimuli that allow participants to project their subjective or deep-seated beliefs onto other people or objects. According to Donoghue (2000), projective techniques can help uncover a person's innermost thoughts and feelings and are based on the idea that subconscious desires and feelings can be explored by presenting a participant with an unthreatening situation in which the participant is free to interpret and respond to the stimuli. Projective techniques and similar elicitation devices are commonly used in qualitative research to gain a deep understanding of a phenomenon (Boddy, 2005).

Unlike stimuli used in other types of research—for example, you can think of a survey as a type of *stimulus* in that it triggers respondents to do something such as select an answer from a limited number of options—the stimuli used in projective techniques are less structured and more effective at getting around consumers' built-in censoring devices. This makes them particularly useful for uncovering honest information about topics that might be sensitive or embarrassing. They are also useful for uncovering subtle differences in how consumers feel about products in categories where no obvious differences exist (such as our toilet paper example). Because there are no right or wrong answers, researchers hope that participants will project their real feelings in their answers. Deeply personal emotions are usually shared by human beings across the board (Hollander, 1988). So if planners can tap into these emotions, they might be able to discover the types of insights that lead to successful advertising. *Elicitation devices* are similar to projective techniques; however, they aren't typically aimed at uncovering subconscious thoughts and feelings but, rather, work as "conversation starters" (Boddy, 2005).

With virtually all projective techniques, the benefit is in the discussion that accompanies the use of the stimulus and not in the stimulus per se. The stimulus itself usually serves mainly to help participants collect their thoughts and explain concepts or ideas (Krueger, 1998). Given this aspect, projective techniques are useful in either one-on-one interviewing or group settings, and each context has its advantages and disadvantages (Bengston, 1982). Individual interviews can elicit responses that are untainted by group or peer pressure, but they don't capitalize on the dynamic that group thinking allows: the generation of ideas sparked when one person responds in a way that stimulates the responses of other group members. One-on-one interviews can yield more detailed information, but group interviews are better at uncovering a wider range of ideas. Bengston (1982) also suggests that projective techniques work better in one-on-one interviews due to the ease of administering them and probing responses, as well as their appropriateness for getting at confidential information that a participant might be reluctant to divulge in a group setting. Our feeling is that the pros and cons of using projective techniques and elicitation devices in one-on-one or group settings are largely determined by the phenomenon you're researching.

HISTORY OF PROJECTIVE TECHNIQUES

According to Rabin (1981), "The penchant of man for imposing his own ideas and interpretations upon unstructured stimuli was noted, and occasionally recorded, centuries ago" (p. 1) and was evident as early as the time of Leonardo da Vinci. However, projective techniques are most often associated with the field of psychology, where their use can be traced back to the mid-1800s. These early attempts lacked a systematic means of analysis, however, and it wasn't until the end of the 19th century that psychologists began using projective techniques in a more rigorous fashion. These early attempts largely concerned the use of inkblots (which came to be known as Rorschach tests), imaginative productions (such as stories told to pictures or other visual cues), and word-association tests (which were first used as instruments for detecting guilt in persons suspected of crimes; Rabin, 1981; Semeonoff, 1976). These early efforts did not become known as projective techniques or projective methods until the late 1930s

(Rabin, 1981); by the 1960s, they were widely embraced by motivational researchers (Robertson & Joselyn, 1974).

Ernest Dichter, a professional motivational researcher, is often credited with introducing Freudian psychology to market research (Piirto, 1990; Soley, 2010), and in his work as early as the 1930s, we see nascent applications of projective techniques to marketing problems. According to Kassarjian (1974), projective techniques have been used in marketing research since shortly after World War II. The first published report—and most widely cited study—on market research using projective techniques was a study by Mason Haire, a behavioral scientist, in 1950. Haire assessed consumers' attitudes toward a product innovation—Nescafe instant coffee—by presenting shopping lists to two groups of 50 women. The only difference in the two lists was in the coffee product that each contained; one list included Nescafe, and the other included Maxwell House drip coffee. After reviewing the two lists, participants were asked to write a paragraph describing the women to whom each list belonged. The Maxwell House woman was described in more positive terms than the Nescafe woman. The Maxwell House woman was viewed as a "good" housewife, whereas the Nescafe woman was described as "lazy," "sloppy," and not a planner (Fram & Cibotti, 1991). To determine whether the negative attitudes were the result of Nescafe, Haire added a fictitious convenience product and repeated the test. The results from this second round of participants resulted in each woman being viewed unfavorably. Haire attributed the common negative findings to the "prepared-food character" of the products (Fram & Cibotti, 1991). Next, Haire conducted a third phase of the study. He presented the Nescafe list to 50 women in their homes, again asking them to write a descriptive paragraph. Coupled with this, researchers administering the stimulus asked to look in the participants' pantries to see whether they had purchased Nescafe. They found that those who wrote unfavorably about the Nescafe woman didn't have Nescafe in their pantries. Conversely, those who were more favorable toward the Nescafe woman also tended to use the product (Fram & Cibotti, 1991).

Until relatively recently, the use of projective techniques by academic researchers has been sporadic and nonuniform, mainly due to questions of validity and reliability (Soley, 2010). Nevertheless, projective techniques have become popular in market research. One reason is their cost efficiency—it often costs much less to use projective techniques in the context of interviewing than it does to conduct segmentation studies that might not yield the same quality information. Most agencies now report that they use projective techniques more frequently and segmentation studies less. However, market parity also might be a reason for the resurgence of these techniques, especially in the advertising industry. According to Piirto (1990), "As consumer spending choices increase, the agency's job of finding the selling hook becomes a search for nuances" (p. 33). Because there's often little that distinguishes competing brands in the eyes of consumers, planners look for small, subtle differences that they might leverage into successful advertising.

TYPES OF PROJECTIVE TECHNIQUES

Any projective technique has two basic aspects. The first is the stimulus, and the second is the participants' responses to the stimulus relative to the meaning the stimulus or situation holds for them (Rabin, 1981). Projective techniques have been categorized in terms of the responses required from participants. Donoghue (2000) offers a typology of projective techniques that divides them into five different categories: association, construction, completion, expressive, and choice ordering. This typology is useful for helping to explain the differences between the various techniques and, we hope, better illustrates the wide variety of projective techniques available to planners. First, however, a note of caution is in order: A lot of books have been written about projective techniques and can be found in the psychology section of the library or your local bookstore. They'll give you a lot of examples of projective techniques. Just be aware that you can seldom translate these examples directly to the type of research you'll be doing and you'll need to make adjustments to some established scales in order to answer whatever your question is. Or you might not find a projective technique that fits what you want to get at, so you might find yourself inventing your own technique (you'll see from the examples below that many ad agencies have done this and even have trademarked their efforts). The thing to keep in mind is that using any projective technique requires skill on the part of the planner. Like conducting interviews, you usually have to use projective techniques a couple of times before you feel comfortable administering them. Also, if your situation requires that you modify or invent your own technique, we strongly urge you to verify the results of your research by triangulating them with other methods until you feel confident that your approach is actually tapping into whatever it is you want to study. We'll talk more about different approaches to triangulation that incorporate projective techniques at the end of this chapter.

Association

In *association* techniques, participants are given a stimulus and are asked to respond with the first words, images, or thoughts that come to mind. The actual response, the speed with which participants answer, and the frequency of a particular response may all be useful tools for understanding the consumer's relationship with a particular brand or product.

One of the most commonly known and oldest forms of association techniques used in marketing research is word association. Word associations have been used by psychologists since the 1880s and have been linked with marketing since World War II. In word associations, respondents are asked to respond with the first word that comes to mind after reading each word in a list or series of words (Donoghue, 2000; Stevens, Wrenn, Ruddick, & Sherwood, 1997).

To veil your motive and not clue in participants to the actual brand or product being tested, the list often includes "neutral" words—those having nothing to do with the brand (e.g., *carrot*, *dog*, *pencil*, etc.)—and "key" words that are directly related to the brand (Kassarjian, 1974). In the latter case, think of coffee as an example. Key words for coffee might include *aroma*, *flavor*, *Folgers*, and *brown*. If you go back to the toilet paper example we gave you at the beginning of this chapter, you might come up with a list that includes key words such as *angel*, *soft*, *clouds*, and *white*. A related associative technique is brand personification. This approach requires participants to associate a brand or product with a person or personality type. Participants are given photographs of different people and are asked to select those that personify either the brand

A group of advertising students working on a class project for Slim Fast's website identified the brand's two main competitors as Jenny Craig and Weight Watchers. To get an idea of what women in the target market thought of the three brands, the students conducted a focus group that incorporated a projective technique. The students asked the participants to draw how the three brands would look if each were a person. The drawings were remarkably similar across the participants. Based on the drawings and the questions asked about the meanings behind the pictures, the students concluded that Jenny Craig was the most upscale brand because the pictures the participants drew of the brand reflected stylish women who were nearing middle age. Similarly, the images that personified Weight Watchers also showed middle-aged women, although they tended to be overweight and not as upscale as the Jenny Craig women. In contrast, the pictures participants drew of Slim Fast showed younger, thin, active women. Coupled with other information gained through the focus group, the students concluded that women in the target market viewed Slim Fast as being for younger and more active women, compared with its main competitors. This insight was later reflected in the positioning strategy used in the campaign the students developed.

Please draw how you think the following brands would like if they were a person.

- Weight Watchers
- Slim Fast
- Jenny Craig

under consideration or its competitors (or, in some instances, both). If photographs are not available, participants can draw the persons they think personify the different brands.

Word associations can help you elicit a consumer vocabulary or list of words commonly associated with brands or products. This vocabulary list is useful for uncovering a brand's identity or its salient product attributes and may ultimately become part of the creative strategy or the resulting advertisements. Similarly, brand personifications help discover the images that consumers hold of a brand and its competitors. Other uses for word associations and similar techniques include assessing trade name recognition and examining the effects of advertising slogans or promotions (Kassarjian, 1974).

To generate a list of key words for an established brand, it is useful to start by looking at past promotional efforts, because these might yield the best trigger words to elicit a response in your participants and help you zero in on important terms. If your goal is to reposition your brand or if your product is new on the market, you might want to start by trying to generate a list of key terms associated with your competitors. Knowing what your brand is (and what it is not) will help determine whether creative strategies should reinforce the brand's image or try to change it.

Association techniques are widely used in advertising. For instance, BBDO Worldwide actually has trademarked its brand personification technique, called Photosort (Piirto, 1990). Using this technique, consumers express their feelings about brands by looking at photos of different types of people. Respondents are then asked to make connections between brands and the pictures of people, with the idea that certain types of people personify the users of certain brands and that by making these matches, an account planner can get an idea of a brand's personality. For example, research conducted for General Electric suggested that consumers thought the brand was conservative and attracted older types. General Electric subsequently changed this image with the help of its "We Bring Good Things to Life" campaign (Piirto, 1990).

Construction

Construction techniques require participants to construct a story or picture from a stimulus concept. These techniques require more

FIGURE 5.1

While it's not a projection technique, another useful way to get a handle on the language associated with your brand is to use a text cloud or "word cloud." Word clouds utilize text and convert it into a visual that looks like a cloud. Words that appear most frequently in text appear the largest in the cloud. This gives you an idea of the most prominent language associated with the text (or, by extension, your brand). This technique was famously used to visualize the content of Barack Obama's inaugural speech compared with those of several past presidents. Looking at Obama's cloud reveals few truly prominent words, suggesting that the speech was somewhat general in nature (Figure 5.1). However, George W. Bush's second inaugural speech clearly displayed a focus on *freedom*, *liberty*, *America*, and *country* (Kirkpatrick, 2009).

Several popular online sites for generating word clouds include wordle.net, tagcrowd.com, and tagxedo.com. We took the text from the previous paragraph and generated a word cloud using wordle.net. The most prominent words were *cloud*, *speech*, and *text*.

While word clouds are useful in identifying the vocabulary associated with a phenomenon, a word of caution is in order. What's being portrayed is frequency and prominence—these tools are devoid of context, so unless you read the text yourself, you risk overlooking important things. Think of word clouds as a place to start—not end—your research.

complex and controlled intellectual activity than do mere associations because the consumer must take a somewhat abstract association and flesh it out (Donoghue, 2000). Participants in a focus group can be asked to develop and present a collage centered on a topic assigned by the planner. The moderator of the focus group can divide the group into two or three smaller teams, each with at least two people.

Allow about 15 to 30 minutes for participants to prepare their displays. Supply resources that will let them add their own words and pictures to the materials you've given them. We've found that access to colored pens or crayons, extra pads of paper, and even retail catalogs (don't forget the scissors!) or dictionaries can often help participants better construct a collage about their feelings.

After participants have completed the collages, you should have each team present its work and encourage feedback and participation from other members of the group (Krueger, 1998).

A similar constructive technique used by planners involves the use of "bubble" drawings or cartoon tests. Participants are provided with actual visuals or cartoons of people portrayed in situations of interest to the planner. Participants are then asked to fill in the bubbles (much like the ones you see in cartoon strips) to indicate what a character is thinking, feeling, or saying in the portrayed situation (Donoghue, 2000). These types of exercises are particularly useful when investigating in-store consumer behavior. For example, if you wanted to know how college students decide among various brands of detergent, you could prepare a visual that shows a young college-aged woman and her roommate standing in the middle of the detergent aisle. The image would show three thought bubbles to illustrate what each of the women is thinking, saying, and feeling.

What the planner is most interested in when using construction techniques is the *process* that participants go through in constructing meaning, rather than the end result that the process yields. Understandably, these techniques require that planners either question participants continually as they complete the exercise or immediately on completion of the exercise so that none of the emotion the participant goes through while making the construction is lost.

Construction techniques work well in both focus groups and one-on-one interviews; however, the complexity of the task you are asking participants to perform will give you some idea of whether it's appropriate for your specific situation. For example, asking a participant in a one-on-one interview to construct a collage is likely to eat up quite a bit of your interview time. This same task in a group setting, however, is much more manageable and is a better use of your time.

Completion

Completion techniques are comparable to word associations in that they tap into similar variables, but they are often considered a bit easier to work with because they better indicate a subject's attitudes and feelings and give good insight into a participant's need-value system (Kassarjian, 1974). With completion techniques, participants are given incomplete sentences, stories, or conversations, or are presented with arguments, and then are asked to complete them. Though this technique can be useful if you have only a limited amount of time with a participant, it requires that you probe participants thoroughly in order to interpret correctly the information they're giving (Donoghue, 2000).

Kassarjian (1974) notes that most market researchers typically phrase completion questions in either the first person (e.g., "When I think of toilet paper, _____.") or the third person (e.g., "When people think of toilet paper, _____." "The average person who thinks about toilet paper _____.").

Care should be taken when constructing a completion stimulus because it heavily influences the type of information an interview will generate. When phrased in the third person, completion techniques are highly useful for gaining insight to participants' deep-seated feelings that might be perceived as negative and are, therefore, hard for a researcher to access. For example, let's say that you are working on behalf of a travel industry client that sells safari packages. You could ask a group of participants whether they might consider Africa as a vacation destination (e.g., "I would go to Africa for a vacation because _____." "I would go to Africa for a vacation if _____.") and, if so, why. We're pretty sure they'd say something along the lines of "the scenery is breathtaking" or "there are a lot of interesting cultures in Africa." But what do you think they'd say if you asked them why a neighbor might consider Africa for a vacation (e.g., "My neighbor would go to Africa for a vacation because _____." "My neighbor would go to Africa for a vacation if _____.")? Chances are you might hear things like "he (or she) likes to show off" or "Africa is where all our friends go on vacation, so he'd go because he has to go to keep up with the Joneses." These latter two are the real reasons your participants might be considering Africa, and giving them the opportunity to talk about someone else—such as their neighbors—enables them to talk freely about attitudes they don't necessarily want to admit they hold.

Completion techniques are useful in either one-on-one or group interviewing and are easily administered; generally, the same procedures are followed for both interview types. For example, in a focus group, the planner can pose a sentence to be completed and then give participants a few minutes to finish the task. As a way of promoting discussion, the planner might read the partial sentence and begin asking participants to give their answers and talk about what they were thinking as they completed the task (obviously, you won't have the benefit of the group discussion if you're doing an individual interview). After all participants have had an opportunity to contribute, the planner might ask for their comments, observations, and opinions about what they saw as similar or different in the answers (Krueger, 1998).

Expressive

Expressive techniques require participants to role-play, act out, tell a story about, draw, or paint a specific concept or situation (Donoghue, 2000). Role-playing is one expressive technique that works particularly well in situations where participants cannot describe their actions or behaviors in an abstract way but can demonstrate them (Krueger, 1998). This technique can be used in either individual interviews or in group situations; it is particularly effective in the latter. According to Krueger (1998), in the context of a focus group, "role-playing is helpful in finding out about complex human interactions through demonstrations" (p. 80). In the focus group, the role-playing activity usually occurs with one or two of the members assuming roles and the rest of the group serving as an audience. Krueger notes that the researcher has a dual opportunity to gather data in this type of situation: She can observe firsthand the outcome of the role-playing, and she has the added opportunity for feedback from the rest of the group.

In addition to role-playing, other expressive techniques are available for account planners. The most widely used expressive technique in both clinical and marketing research is the Thematic Apperception Test, or TAT (Kassarjian, 1974). When used in marketing research, the TAT is appropriate for such areas as copy testing (words, visuals, and colors); gaining insight into qualities associated with different products and the people who use them; and exploring attitudes toward products, brands, images of institutions, or symbols. The TAT consists of a series of pictures or cartoons on cards that convey the research topic but are presented in a situation that is somewhat ambiguous. Standardized TAT visuals have been developed over the years, or a researcher might come up with her own. If you develop your own visuals, ambiguity (how much a participant can read into a visual—it should be sufficiently ambiguous to elicit a number of stories but focused enough to help answer your research question), the content of the visual, and how elements of the visual are arranged all need to be considered (Soley & Smith, 2008). When using the TAT, participants are asked to review the image and construct a story about what they see (Donoghue, 2000). They may also be asked to elaborate on what led to the portrayed scene and what might happen in the future. Themes are developed based on the participants' personal interpretations of the pictures (Zikmund, 1984). Major themes are then analyzed across participants to uncover their subconscious feelings and motivations (Soley, 2006).

Expressive techniques have been used successfully to discover things about consumers. For example, to find out how teenagers feel about acne for its client Clearasil, D'Arcy Masius Benton & Bowles used a TAT. After being shown a picture of a person who had a blemish, the teenagers were asked to describe the feelings of the person in the picture. The agency found that to teenagers, pimples mean social isolation and being different. As a result, the agency developed a campaign to let teens know that they could get back into life quickly if they used Clearasil. According to a spokesperson for the agency, "We wouldn't have gotten that kind of information if we simply asked them to talk about acne and acne remedies" (Piirto, 1990, p. 33).

As with most other projective techniques, the visual must be interesting enough to promote discussion but not so obvious as to give away the purpose of your research. The visual also must be relevant to the participants. By way of illustrating these last two points, Zikmund (1984) relates the story of a research project conducted on why men purchase chain saws. A visual of a man looking at a large tree was used to explore buying motives among homeowners and weekend woodcutters. The participants' initial reaction to the visual was that it wasn't a job for them but required the help of a professional. In other words, they couldn't relate to the man with the problem, so they didn't consider sawing down the tree themselves as part of the solution. Similarly, when deciding on the stimulus to use in a TAT, the planner should refrain from giving clues that indicate an obvious positive or negative predisposition to any elements of the visual.

"The House Where the Brand Lives" (or variations thereof) is another common expressive technique used by planners. Planners may introduce a series of brands one by one and then ask the participant to describe the exterior of a house where each of the brands lives. What style of house is it? Is it big? Small? Run-down? Well kept? Does it have a porch? How about a yard? What's in the yard? Carrying it a little further, you can also ask the participants to describe the person who answers the door of the house, others who may live in the house, and what the individual rooms look like. To get insight into media use habits, you might also inquire about the channels to which the TV is tuned, what magazine subscriptions the residents of the home have, to what station the radio in the kitchen is tuned, and so on. This technique offers great insight into a brand's image among consumers and may suggest opportunities in the marketplace.

A beer example offers a good illustration of this. We asked students in an advertising class to describe the houses where two brands of beer—Rolling Rock and Budweiser—lived. Although Budweiser has the larger market share, both beers are domestics that are nationally distributed and equitably priced, so they appear to share many similarities. The students described the house where Budweiser "lived" as middle-class and probably located in an older suburb. The house was not large but was well kept. There was a yard with a well-kept lawn. In the yard were toys, suggesting that a family lived there. The man who answered the door was in his 30s and casually dressed, a white-collar worker enjoying a weekend at home. The living room was traditional, containing a sofa and a couple of easy chairs; it was clean but definitely lived-in (toys strewn about, etc.). The living room contained a widescreen television that was tuned to ESPN, where a football game was in progress.

Now, contrast this image with the one students constructed for the Rolling Rock home: It was smaller and a bit run-down, possibly in a city. The yard was weedy with a lot of bare spots; in the driveway were a couple of cars, none new (our students called them "beaters"). The home had a porch; on the porch was an old couch. A knock on the door was also answered by a man, but this man had on a T-shirt with a couple of stains; he was a blue-collar worker. The man looked as though he may have been woken by the knock on the door. His living room also contained a couch and a couple of chairs, but they were a bit threadbare. From the looks of his home, he lived alone. He had a television, but it wasn't widescreen. The television was tuned to a wrestling match on WTBS.

What conclusions can you draw from the above descriptions concerning the brand images of these two beers? An obvious one is that the image of Budweiser was a bit more upscale than that of Rolling Rock. Looking deeper into the data, you could conclude that Budweiser is a more mainstream beer, middle-class, and the beer of choice for a "regular" guy. In contrast, Rolling Rock is a much more blue-collar beer. And that's not necessarily a bad thing, considering that Rolling Rock beer has its own niche in the market and does quite well. But the students' descriptions certainly describe two different images, both of which might certainly influence creative strategy (e.g., these descriptions suggest that it would be hard to position either of these beers as the beverage of choice for the sophisticated man).

Choice Ordering

Donoghue (2000) notes that *choice ordering* techniques are frequently used in quantitative research but can also be used informally in qualitative research. Techniques of this type require participants to explain why certain things are more important than others. After presenting a stimulus that asks participants to rank a list of product benefits from *most important* to *least important*, a planner will use probing questions to find out why participants designated some benefits as more important than others. Choice ordering techniques are also useful when you want participants to rank or order characteristics associated with a product, brand, or service (Donoghue, 2000). This information can be used to develop creative strategy or to reposition a brand.

Perceptual Mapping

Perceptual maps are an ideal way to get folks talking, most effectively in the context of a group interview. A *perceptual map* is a graphic technique that attempts to visually display the perceptions of participants relative to several dimensions of a product or brand (Hausman, 2010). While perceptual maps are often used in quantitative research to develop multidimensional scales or discriminate among entities being compared on multiple attributes (Teas & Grapentine, 2004), they are also useful in qualitative research. For example, if you know how consumers view your client's product relative to that of its competitors on key dimensions, you can more easily develop brand and competitive strategies, recognize areas in which your brand is struggling, identify areas for potential product line extensions, or pinpoint consumer segments in a market not currently being served (Ganesh & Oakenfull, 1999; Hausman, 2010). Sounds like a great tool, huh?

We asked students in our campaigns class to evaluate five fast-food restaurants (Burger King, Krystal, McDonald's, Taco Bell, and Wendy's) along two dimensions: value (good vs. bad) and variety (a lot vs. a little). Executing the exercise was simple enough—on the blackboard, we drew a horizontal line and labeled the endpoints "good value" and "bad value." We wrote the names of the five brands on Post-it Notes so we could easily move them around as the discussion unfolded. Then we asked the students, "Where do you think Burger King should be positioned on the line in terms of value?" Immediately, the students wanted to know what we meant by value. Were we talking about cost? Quality of the food? We responded by telling them that we were interested in what value meant to them relative to each of the brands. The discussion became quite lively, with aspects such as cost, quality of products, and hours of operation (our students thought a restaurant open at 3 a.m. was quite valuable!) all provoking interesting conversation. As researchers, our goal wasn't to reach consensus in the discussion but mainly to keep the conversation going and to probe various aspects of value as they came up (e.g., "Can you tell more about that?" "Does anyone else feel that way?"). Before we moved on to the next brand, we would gently say, "Well, it looks like the majority of you think _____ should be about here on the line. Now let's talk about the next restaurant."

When the discussion of value wound down, we drew a vertical line down the middle of the value line. We labeled this new line with endpoints of "a lot of variety" and "little variety." Then we asked the students if the various brands should be moved up or down along that line. Again, this sparked a lot of conversation, and subjects we didn't think about emerged. For instance, Taco Bell—a restaurant with a pretty extensive menu—was perceived as having less variety than some of the other brands because, "sure, there's a lot of things, but they're all made with the same ingredients." McDonald's fared the best on this dimension because it offered a lot of different options but it also served three meals, which to the students was an aspect of variety. Wendy's, which has a more limited menu with fewer value-menu items, and doesn't serve breakfast, ranked at the bottom of the variety line.

So what is this one telling us? Lots of things. McDonald's pretty much owns its quadrant and is perceived as a good-value restaurant with lots of variety. This suggests that McDonald's strategy of the past few years of adding specialty coffees and menu items such as oatmeal seems to be working. As the market leader, McDonald's would want to defend and continue with this position. On the other end of the spectrum, Krystal is a brand perceived as a somewhat

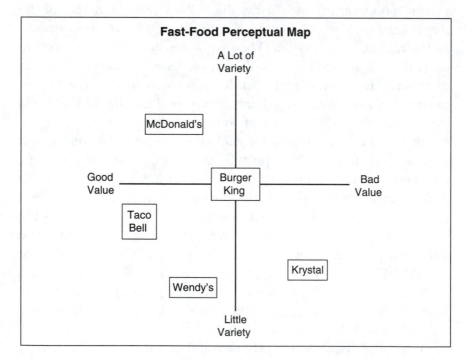

FIGURE 5.2

Figure 5.2 gives you an idea of where our discussion ended up and what a perceptual map looks like.

bad value with not so much variety (Krystal is open 24 hours, and our students seemed to think it was a good idea only at 3 a.m.). One thing Krystal might try is to introduce new products that go beyond hamburgers. It might also implement a communication strategy aimed at educating consumers about its 24-hour convenience and inexpensive menu items. Burger King seems to have little "personality" relative to the dimensions of value and variety; it's neither good nor bad. If Burger King does, indeed, have value and variety, all that might be in order is a retooling of its communication strategy to focus on aspects of the two dimensions, along with possible line extensions or new product introductions.

We think this example gives you some idea of the value of perceptual mapping, particularly the discussion it invokes. Again, when used in a qualitative manner, this technique elicits from the participants associations that the clients or planners might not have considered. This information could be used in a variety of ways, including in advertising.

A couple of cautions accompany perceptual maps. Visually, portraying more than two dimensions on a map is difficult, and the dimensions you select as your endpoints must be selected carefully. Hausman (2010) notes that these dimensions should be based on something that determines which products consumers purchase. To this, we would add that the dimensions should not be too factual or concrete. In the above example, if we used "price" instead of "value," our data would not have been nearly as rich.

ADVANTAGES AND DISADVANTAGES OF PROJECTIVE TECHNIQUES

The primary disadvantage of using projective and elicitation techniques is the complexity of the data and the skills required to analyze the data (Boddy, 2005). This is especially true for those who are not familiar with qualitative data analysis. Nevertheless, qualitative data analysis is a *learned* skill and one that becomes easier the more often you do it. Because of the complexity of the task, many planners opt to hire out research requiring the use of projective techniques. That leads to another disadvantage: The use of interviewers skilled in administering and analyzing projective techniques is often expensive. However, even if a planner opts to hire out research incorporating these techniques, the planner still needs to understand their utility and have some idea of data analysis in order to evaluate the quality of the outside researcher's work. We discuss different approaches to analyzing data from these techniques at the end of this chapter; the data analysis techniques we recommend are essentially those that apply to most qualitative research and were discussed earlier in this book.

Donoghue (2000) points out that insights generated by projective techniques are usually not considered to be representative of a larger population because the samples often aren't large enough to perform tests that have statistical significance. However, the types of insights planners are looking for begin with consumers themselves, and a single comment by one individual might lead to the sought-after insight. If necessary, that insight can later be followed up with a larger number of consumers.

The nature of some projective techniques also calls into question the reliability and validity of what is being measured. Reliability refers to the idea that a good research measure yields data that are stable (e.g., the likelihood that you'll see similar results if you perform the same research with a like group of participants). Validity refers to whether the technique is measuring what it is supposed to measure. In other words, how do you know that the bubble cartoon a participant filled in reflects what the participant feels? The issues of reliability and validity associated with projective data often have led to criticism of their use. However, a study by Ramsey, Ibbotson, and McCole (2006) aimed at assessing the value of projective techniques concluded that they are, indeed, reliable and valid approaches that provide valuable insight.

Another disadvantage of projective techniques is that getting participants to take part in them may be difficult. For example, some subjects might refuse to participate or be uncomfortable participating in such activities as role-playing exercises. Administering and encouraging participation in these types of research techniques often requires a skilled interviewer.

Despite their limitations, projective techniques offer many advantages. The main advantage is the amount, richness, and accuracy of information that can be collected (Donoghue, 2000). This is especially true in cases where the focus of study is a person's beliefs, values, motivations, personality, or other unique behaviors (such as product purchases!), which are not easily measured or uncovered using more traditional research methods.

Projective techniques are also useful in the context of a focus group for stimulating discussion or breaking the ice. Participants tend to enjoy projective techniques, and they can inflect new energy into a focus group and lighten the mood of the research (Donoghue, 2000).

Projective techniques are a good way to get truthful responses from participants, because participants often aren't sure what you're trying to measure and don't feel as though they are at risk of giving socially unacceptable answers. And, even if they are aware of the general purpose of the research, they often aren't quite sure what aspects a planner is interested in. Because the tasks that participants are called on to do are more free-form and unstructured than traditional research approaches, participants do not perceive their answers as right or wrong and can be easily encouraged to respond with a wide range of ideas (Donoghue, 2000). Also, projective techniques require little in the way of literacy skills, which widens their scope beyond what might be included in a survey or measured via an experiment. This lack of literacy requirements also makes some projective techniques particularly appropriate for children or other populations that are unable or unwilling to articulate their feelings using written words.

DATA ANALYSIS

You might think it's your job to interpret data generated from projective techniques, but it's actually the job of the participants, with the help of your guidance (Krueger, 1998). Nevertheless, ideas rarely come directly from consumers, so a planner needs to develop the skills to make connections that will uncover marketplace opportunities.

According to Donoghue (2000), there are two approaches to analyzing projective data. The first is to approach the data quantitatively, whereby the planner classifies the content into categories that are given numerical values. The specific categories can then be tabulated and used to evaluate a subject's responses or the frequency of responses by groups.

For example, let's say you're conducting research on coffee. You might look over the answers participants gave on the projective tests you conducted and group the answers dealing with color or the visual aspects of coffee (e.g., dark brown, cream colored, rich looking) into a category titled "Appearance." Then, after categorizing all the participants' answers in this way, you might find that coffee's appearance was cited often by participants and conclude that appearance is important to consumers. In and of itself, that finding isn't going to be important unless you know *why*. Although quantitative analysis of the answers may be useful in tasks such as uncovering the frequency of certain responses, looking at "top-of-the-mind" characteristics of a product, or trying to plot a conceptual map based on consumer opinions and attitudes, it often doesn't result in the types of insights planners tend to seek. As we mentioned before, it's important to consider the answers participants give in context. You should be aware that using any of the projective techniques we've discussed in this chapter requires a great deal of follow-up questioning and probing on the part of the planner to establish the context of the answer and give it meaning.

As noted in Chapter 2, computers are another option for data analysis and are sometimes useful tools for organizing projective data. Several computer programs on the market, including NUD*IST and ETHNOGRAPH, are widely embraced by researchers looking for a systematic way of analyzing qualitative data. Other agencies use proprietary programs developed in-house. In fact, several agencies actually have trademarked computer programs that they developed for data analysis. For example, the Leo Burnett advertising agency has developed what it calls the Emotional Lexicon, "an interactive computerized system that studies emotions derived from product categories" (Piirto, 1990, p. 35). This computerized system leads a participant through an interview containing certain key words or phrases developed to represent a number of different emotional dimensions that can be reduced to 15 key points. According to a Leo Burnett spokesperson, these data enable the agency to pinpoint whether consumers develop product preferences based on emotional or rational choices.

The second approach to analyzing projective data is qualitative analysis. Qualitative analysis and interpretation of projective data are really no different from how qualitative data are usually analyzed. As opposed to categorizing the data by numbers, qualitative data analysis is much more focused on trying to uncover patterns in the data that give insight to what lies behind or what is meant by the projections. Krueger (1998) recommends a two-part strategy that involves both participant assistance and multiple data sources to analyze the data gathered from projective techniques. He recommends that you begin by asking participants exactly what their answers mean and what part of an answer you should focus on. In other words, what's the important part of what they're really saying? As you ask this question of more and more participants (either over the course of several focus groups or as you continue conducting interviews), you should begin to see response patterns emerge. As these patterns solidify, you'll gain confidence that the answers you're seeing are actually the way the target market feels about whatever issue you're looking at.

The second part of Krueger's (1998) recommended strategy deals with trying to see if you can get the same patterns of data to emerge using more than one method. He notes that projective techniques are but one aspect of reality and should be checked against other ways of getting at the answers to the questions you're asking. In academe, we call this approach triangulation, which is a fancy way of saying that different methods of looking at the same problem and asking the same questions should yield similar results. So you might use a combination of projective techniques to see if you arrive at similar answers, or you might try another combination of methods. This can often be done with the same group of participants in the same session.

For example, a study conducted by Market Research Organization for Commercial Market Strategies sought to explore women's attitudes about different forms of contraception (Commercial Market Strategies, 2001; NOP Research Group, 2001). To do so, the agency conducted research among three groups of women of reproductive age who were selected based on demographic characteristics and familiarity with a range of contraceptive methods. Each participant was interviewed individually and was asked to read a brief medical record about a fictitious young woman with three children. There was only one difference in the account the women in each group read: the fictitious woman's method of contraception. The women in one group were told that the woman had undergone a surgical procedure to prevent conception, women in the second group were told that she used the rhythm method, and women in the last group read that she used an IUD (or intrauterine device). After reading the account, the women were asked to talk about the woman in the medical record: What kind of family life did she have? What kind of wife and mother was she? Did the participants see her as risky or conservative? Was she modern or traditional? The participants were also asked to indicate how much they agreed or disagreed with a similar set of statements about the woman in the record.

After these data were analyzed, the results indicated that the three groups had very different impressions of the fictitious woman. Because the only thing that varied in the accounts the three groups read was the method of contraception, their answers offered interesting insights into how they viewed the three forms of contraception. The participants viewed the woman who had the surgical procedure negatively: She was seen as uneducated, in poor health, living in poverty, and largely indifferent to the needs of her family. The group who read that the woman used the rhythm method for contraception viewed her as old-fashioned and unreliable, decent but out of the mainstream. She was also seen as a risk taker because her contraception method was unreliable. The woman who used the IUD, in contrast, was well regarded by the women who read her story. She was viewed as modern and a good mother and wife. She was also considered stable, well educated, and conservative (because her contraceptive method had been around awhile and was trusted).

This example serves to drive home the importance of triangulation. Three different ways of getting respondents to answer the question were used: traditional one-on-one interviewing and two projective techniques (expressive and choice ordering). Separately, they all suggested the same thing about the participants' views of contraception. But taken together, the different approaches reinforced the patterns the researchers were seeing and also helped flesh out the answers better than if only one method had been used. As with all data analysis, the key is to try to see whether the patterns that emerge are valid—that is, whether they're really answering what you're trying to answer—and similar despite the different approaches. It's kind of like not putting all your eggs in one basket.

SUMMARY

Projective techniques involve the use of stimuli that allow participants to project their subjective or deep-seated beliefs onto other people or objects. The general idea behind these techniques is that a researcher can explore subconscious desires and feelings by presenting participants with unthreatening situations which they interpret and to which they respond.

Projective techniques are extremely useful for uncovering honest information about topics that might be sensitive or embarrassing, or for uncovering subtle differences in how consumers feel about products in categories where no obvious differences exist.

Any projective technique has two basic aspects: the stimulus and the response to the stimulus. Projective techniques can be grouped into categories such as association, construction, completion, expressive, and choice ordering.

Projective techniques are used in the process of interviewing and are usually appropriate for either one-on-one or group interviews.

Projective techniques come with advantages and disadvantages. The main advantages are the amount, richness, and accuracy of the information that can be collected; its usefulness for stimulating discussion; and its ability to elicit responses to sensitive questions. The main disadvantages are the complexity of the data and the high level of skill required for a planner to analyze the data, as well as questions about the reliability and validity of data the techniques yield.

At this point, you're probably getting a better idea of why planners are often called creative researchers. In the next chapter, we shift our focus to another innovative way to gather information about consumers—online! If you think that conducting interviews and focus groups through the Internet or e-mail can help you tap into consumer insights, then we've got some great ideas you can use. Read on.

KEY TERMS

association: Projective technique in which participants are given a stimulus and then asked to respond with the first words, images, or thoughts that come to mind.

choice ordering: Projective technique that requires participants to explain why certain things are more important than others. Participants are given a stimulus and then asked to rank order a list of associated benefits or features from *most important* to *least important*.

completion: Projective technique in which participants are given incomplete sentences, stories, or conversations, or are presented with arguments, and then asked to complete them.

construction: Projective technique that requires participants to construct a story or picture from a stimulus concept. Construction techniques require more complex and controlled intellectual activity than do mere associations.

elicitation devices: Any object or activity used in the context of individual or group interviews that gets participants talking. These differ from projective techniques in that they aren't typically focused on attitudes and feelings that participants hold on a subconscious level.

expressive: Projective technique in which participants are required to role-play, act out, tell a story about, draw, or paint a specific concept or situation.

perceptual map: A graphic technique that attempts to visually display the perceptions of participants relative to several dimensions of a product or brand.

projective techniques: Psychological approaches involving the use of stimuli that allow participants to project their subjective or deep-seated beliefs onto other people or objects. The general idea behind these techniques is that subconscious desires and feelings can be explored by presenting a participant with a stimulus in an unthreatening situation so the participant is free to interpret and respond to the stimulus.

stimulus: Object used in projective techniques to which the participant responds. Common stimuli for advertising research include collages, brand names, trademarks, slogans, and commercials.

EXERCISES

1.   Select a product category that has several well-known competitors. Form a group of three or four of your classmates or peers. Ask the members of the group to draw a picture of a person to personify each brand. Make sure they do this individually. Tell them to draw as well as they can, but stress that artistic skills don't matter. When finished, tape the pictures grouped by brand to a wall where all members can see them. Examine the pictures and attempt to identify commonalities among the pictures in each group and differences across groups. Based on your findings, write a description of the person that typifies each brand.

2.   Find an online review site for a product in which you are interested. This should be a site where consumers can leave their evaluations of the product. Examine the comments and identify three that are generally positive and three that are negative. Generate a word cloud by cutting and pasting the positive text into a word cloud program (three that we like are tagcrowd.com, wordle. net, and tagxedo.com). Do the same with the negative language. Examine the resulting clouds and try to identify major and repeating words. Are there any patterns in the language used to assess your brand? What are the most often occurring positive and negative words? What conclusions can you draw about how these consumers feel about the product?

3.   Go to your local grocery store and take a picture of a group of products in the same product category (e.g., if you are interested in cereal, take the picture in the cereal aisle). Make sure to get several different brands in your shot. Then, on a piece of white paper, sketch the back of a person with a cartoon bubble coming from the top of her head. Try to make the person fairly "formless" and without too many identifying characteristics. Paste the person on top of the photo. Make copies and ask several different people to fill in the bubble and tell you what the person in the picture is thinking about. You can carry this one step further by asking your participants to create a story about the scenario: What led the person to be in the cereal aisle? On what basis will she make her decision? Is she buying the

cereal for herself or someone else? What will happen after she takes the cereal home? Make sure you probe the participants about their responses.

RELATED READING

Fortini-Campbell, L. (2001). *Hitting the sweet spot*. Chicago, IL: Copy Workshop.

Rabin, A. I. (1981). *Assessment with projective techniques: A concise introduction*. New York, NY: Springer.

Rotenberg, R. H. (1995). *A manager's guide to marketing research*. Toronto, Ontario Canada: Dryden.

Soley, L., & Smith, A. L. (2008). *Projective techniques for social science and business research*. Milwaukee, WI: Southshore.

Zikmund, W. G. (1997). *Exploring marketing research* (6th ed.). Orlando, FL: Dryden.

6

Qualitative Research Online

FOCUS GROUPS AND INTERVIEWS

The Internet is like our morning coffee or after-work cocktail: It has become part of many people's daily lives. Today, Americans spend time daily on the Internet—checking e-mail, reading headlines, staying connected with friends and family, paying bills, shopping, and more. Given the amount of time spent online, and the seemingly constant conversations happening in the online space, it is not surprising that researchers seek ways to conduct research online as well.

Indeed, a review of the Internet's history suggests that enhanced communication and research were always at the core of its development. The U.S. Department of Defense built ARPANET, the precursor to the Internet, in 1969 as a way to link distinct groups such as universities and research contractors (Goldring, 1997). The National Science Foundation took over responsibility for the Internet in the 1980s and promoted it as a way for all manner of researchers and academics to collaborate and share information. Hand in hand with this institutional development were changes that enhanced opportunities for individuals to be part of this networked society.

The National Science Foundation relinquished control over a major part of the Internet in 1993 and sanctioned its use for commercial purposes. The World Wide Web, originally developed at the Swiss research lab CERN, blossomed and grew with the new range of commercial possibilities. Today, this communication power is harnessed by advertising agencies not only to advertise products and services but also to research and communicate with consumers.

Today, it is difficult to find anyone in the United States who does not have access to the Internet. Worldwide, more than 2 billion people have Internet access, with these numbers increasing every day due to the proliferation of smartphones in developing countries. On average, an Internet user is online via a computer about an hour each day. However, the proliferation of other types of devices such as mobile phones and tablet computers, such as iPads, means that online access is much more portable than ever before. As a result, many Americans are constantly wired, and many account planners look to the Internet to collect consumer information.

To date, account planners have implemented both quantitative and qualitative research online. For example, account planners have conducted quantitative surveys online using both e-mail and web-based data collection methods, with varying degrees of success. One attractive feature of the Internet is the potential for obtaining a large number of responses quickly. For numerous reasons, however, account planners have difficulty determining the generalizability of such surveys. These reasons include the possibility that a single individual could provide multiple responses to a single survey and that responses could be collected from individuals not in the target audience (e.g., children under the age of 18 could respond to online surveys focused on adult products). There isn't any single source, like the U.S. census, that can accurately provide a good picture of the actual demographic makeup of the Internet population, either in the United States or worldwide (Mann & Stewart, 2000). Without such a source, the ability to generate a random sample, which is so important in quantitative research, is diminished.

Implementing qualitative research programs online has become popular among consumer researchers. As with quantitative research, data can be collected quickly from individuals around the world. Moreover, the generalizability issues associated with quantitative research are not as germane to qualitative research. Two specific types of qualitative research—focus groups and depth interviews—are seen as particularly fitting for the Internet environment. In this chapter, we focus on the use of focus groups and depth interviews online. We describe the types of focus groups and depth interviews that can be conducted online and discuss the pros and cons of each. We also provide guidelines for how best to implement these techniques.

ONLINE FOCUS GROUPS

When you think about a traditional focus group, you probably have a picture in your mind of a group of people of the same gender and roughly the same age sitting around a table with soft drinks and sharing their opinions on a specific topic, product, or service. Take away the table, the soft drinks, and the ability for members of the group to look at one another, and you have an online focus group. What remains is a forum for diverse opinions to be heard.

Harold Bragen (2000), president of ARC Research in Cranford, New Jersey, believes that online focus groups "may constitute the most useful new research technique to appear since the introduction of CATI (computer-assisted telephone interviewing)" (p. 8). Although online focus groups may not be the best choice for all types of advertising and marketing planning research, the technology has many diverse applications. For example, online focus groups can be used to study the following groups:

- *Persons with affinities to different topics.* Because the Internet allows for the development of various communities of interest, recruiting beyond a demographic group is simple. It is possible to find people with highly specific interests—such as knitters, kayakers, or dog groomers—with a click of a mouse.
- *High-level decision makers with busy schedules.* Online focus groups can study how these executives make decisions or use products; such executives are unlikely to travel to a facility to participate in a group yet may be willing to log on to the web for an hour or two to interact with others in their peer group.
- *Hidden populations of persons who may not overtly indicate their membership in a specific group* (e.g., drug users, trauma or violent crime survivors).

- *People who interact, or don't, with online advertising*. Online focus groups can study perceptions of banner advertisements and other online advertising offerings. In fact, every type of web-related topic is a natural subject for online focus groups. Online audiences can quickly assess creative work, particularly in the development stage.
- *Brand advocates*. Online users of social networks such as Facebook have the opportunity to indicate their affinity for brands that set up pages in the social space. These advocates can be sources for strong consumer preferences about your brand.

Obviously, certain types of consumer research won't be feasible online, such as tests comparing taste preferences (e.g., the famous Pepsi Challenge) and tests of a tactile nature (e.g., comparing one type of fabric or paper with another). Beyond this, though, almost any topic that is appropriate for an in-person group may well work with an online group, unless you know that people in your target group are part of that rare category of people who are not web savvy.

Many believe that online focus groups will never replace face-to-face focus groups because the "two are different animals" (Greenbaum, 2000, p. 34). Many research firms see online groups as a complement to, not a replacement for, traditional panels. However, online focus groups offer several benefits over traditional focus groups. One of the biggest benefits is that no geographic barriers prevent participation: People in the group can come from across the country or around the world. In addition, these participants won't have to pay to travel to a focus group facility or incur other costs (such as child care costs) in order to participate in the group. These factors create a huge pool of potential participants from which to select for your focus group. In fact, account planners report that many people won't travel to a facility but may participate in an online group—and higher income persons rarely participate in traditional focus groups.

Researchers can conduct focus groups online in numerous ways, depending on whether they wish the group to be synchronous or asynchronous. A *synchronous group* is one happening in real time: That is, the group operates with a start and end time, just as an in-person focus group would. These tend to occur in a chat room–type format. An *asynchronous group* is one where the conversation occurs anytime and at irregular intervals.

Each of these types of groups (Table 6.1) is handled uniquely, has specific strengths for researchers, and also has some unique challenges.

Synchronous Groups

Synchronous groups, held during a specific time period with clear opening and closing times, can be used in either a text or multimedia format. A text-only group could be held in a *chat room* set up especially for the focus group. A multimedia group, allowing people to see one another during the group meeting, could be held via videoconferencing software or through an online service such as Skype.

Synchronous groups using only text may be more efficient for account planners in terms of cost and time commitment. One of the biggest cost savings comes from lack of facility costs: Because participants do not gather in a facility for the sessions, rental costs for the facility or the travel costs for agency personnel to get to the facility are not accrued. You will save time because you can schedule the online focus groups at your or your client's convenience and do not have to worry about scheduling conflicts at the facility. Transcripts also will be available quickly since participants are typing their dialogue and creating a transcript as the group progresses. A synchronous group using videoconferencing software would be

TABLE 6.1   Types of Online Focus Groups

	Synchronous (Closed-Ended)	*Asynchronous (Open-Ended)*
Text only	Chat rooms	Social networking sites Discussion boards
Multimedia	Videoconference Skype	N/A

somewhat less efficient since participants would likely have to travel to the facility. Setting up software such as Skype on a home computer would eliminate this concern and allow for easy access for a multimedia group.

Because online groups can be implemented quickly, you have the opportunity to quickly pinpoint consumer trends and/or reactions to current events. Also, the responses from online focus groups would possibly be superior to the responses from traditional focus groups. For example, peer pressure is minimized online because participants are engaging in discussions from the privacy of their own environments. Particularly with a text-based group, participants cannot judge one another based on appearance, and a single participant will find it difficult to dominate the conversation, even if he or she is an incredibly fast typist! Not being able to see the panel or hear how they talk minimizes prejudging of the individuals (Weissman, 1998). Because each participant's voice can be "heard," everyone has an equal voice (Weissman, 1998). Without the physical presence of other participants or even a moderator, participants are anonymous and so may be willing to divulge information they might not divulge in a traditional focus group situation.

Video synchronous groups hold most of the same benefits as text-only groups. Additional benefits include the ideas that many respondents may find it easier to respond by speaking than by typing on a keyboard and that richness of communication can be observed. The challenges of recruitment and moderator involvement for text groups hold true for video groups.

Challenges

Participant Identification and Recruitment

In both traditional and online focus groups, participants are likely to be screened for certain demographic and/or psychographic characteristics before the group actually assembles. If you were recruiting for a focus group on fashion-forward, young, working women, for example, you might ask about each participant's age, ethnic background, and the types of clothing she purchases. In a traditional focus group, it would be evident whether the answers participants gave during the prescreening were true when each participant arrived at the facility (i.e., you would be able to tell that they were women, what their ethnic backgrounds were, their approximate ages, etc.). Anyone who did not meet the requirements could be excluded from the group at that time. However, such visual confirmation is not available online in the text format. In fact, it would be possible to recruit for a group of fashion-forward, young, working women and end up with an online group made up of 80-year-old men! Later in this chapter, we review the different ways to recruit for online focus groups and provide recommendations on how best to screen so that who you want is who you get. Keep in mind, though, that there will always be people who misrepresent themselves online. That's a risk we take as online researchers.

Moderator Interaction and the Group Process

One of the hallmarks of traditional focus groups is the presence of a moderator who controls the flow of the discussion. Many critics worry that moderators of online focus groups won't be able to establish authority and keep the group on track (Weissman, 1998). This may be especially problematic in a text-based group. The key to addressing this concern is recognizing that online moderators need a set of skills applicable to the online environment in addition to the traditional group-moderating skills. For example, moderators in both traditional and online groups must determine how much time to devote to each question. In a traditional group, the moderator can orally direct the discussion to the next topic. In an online group, however, the moderator can try to close a discussion and type a question that moves the group to a new topic but could be ignored by the group. The group could continue to discuss the original topic ad infinitum, much to the distress of the moderator. In a similar vein, the moderator must find ways to control any participants who are damaging the group process. Finally, the moderator must make sure that participants stay for the whole session in order to create the best group dynamic. These specific problems are discussed in a later section on the role of the moderator.

Information Richness

Arguably, the greatest difference between traditional and online focus groups, particularly in a text-based group, is the lack of nonverbal cues in the online environment. In a traditional group, much can be inferred from rolling of eyes, sarcastic tones of voice, nodding heads, and other nonverbal cues that accompany the discussion. The lack of nonverbal cues in a text-based online group may limit the comprehension that can be obtained from the discussion. Even in a video group, people may behave differently "on camera" than they do in a live situation and may edit themselves and not provide the same level of visual cues they might in a traditional group.

The lack of nonverbal cues may be a benefit, because an outspoken person may become the focus of the analysis or the discussion in a traditional group interview. As previously mentioned, an online focus group can allow for soft-spoken and quiet people to have the same voice as the others in the group.

In actuality, the lack of nonverbal cues for a text-only group suggests that traditional forms of participant analysis have to be revised when looking at online focus groups. Bragen (2000) suggests that account planners analyzing focus group data use techniques such as close textual analysis or language choice analysis to determine the tone or emotional content of a piece of writing. Therefore, the analysis techniques described earlier in this book can apply to online focus groups.

PLANNING THE GROUP AND THE ROLE OF THE MODERATOR

The upfront planning for an online focus group is identical to the planning for a traditional focus group. Agency and client representatives should meet to discuss exactly what needs to be learned and what is the best way to do so.

For a synchronous group, the moderator should announce that the group is formally in session at the designated time. The moderator then takes control of the proceedings. The moderator should introduce the participants, encourage them to answer any and all questions posed, and for a text-based group, let the participants know that they shouldn't be concerned about spelling and grammar. The moderator can then officially start the focus group.

The qualifications for an online moderator are somewhat similar to those for an offline moderator. The moderator must be a good listener and be able to keep track of all members of the group and encourage their participation. In addition, the moderator for a text-based group should be able to type proficiently, or else have standard questions that can quickly be cut and pasted into dialogue boxes.

Many account planners who have used online text-based focus groups recommend having two moderators. The role of the first moderator, Moderator A, is the same as that of the moderator in a traditional focus group. Moderator A runs the group and is the only moderator interacting with the group. Moderator A is responsible for setting the tone of the group, introducing the participants, and leading the discussion. However, he or she must listen more actively than the traditional moderator. Online listening is expressed in words—not silence, as in an offline conversation. Listening with interest means that Moderator A should respond promptly to participants' questions, express interest in particular points made, and ask follow-up questions that refer directly to the information being presented.

The second moderator, Moderator B, interacts with client and agency personnel observing the group and reads their messages so he or she can advise Moderator A on follow-up questions as well as client or agency concerns. The two moderators should ideally sit side by side so they can communicate verbally with each other; if this is not possible, they can talk via speaker telephone. Moderator B should be alert to changes in the tone of the conversation that might signal that a question was misunderstood or suggest that participants would be happy to talk more about something when asked (Mann & Stewart, 2000). Moderator B also should tell Moderator A which participant wants to provide more information. Moderator A is responsible for handling probes and should be sure to name the participant to whom the probe is directed; otherwise, all members of the group may jump in to answer the question.

Certainly, any of the problems or issues that arise in traditional focus groups can also arise in an online group; however, some different techniques may be necessary to deal with such problems. For example, it is possible that one individual will be the dominant group member: He or she may type the same point repeatedly. Moderator A, using active listening techniques, should confirm that the individual is being heard (e.g., the moderator could type, "Good point, Susan. What do others think about that?"). If the dominating individual is taking the discussion off topic, the moderator should keep repeating the question until it is answered, perhaps naming the individual leading the digression (e.g., "Nancy, those are good points about the product's quality. Let's move on to talk about taste and texture, and if we have time, we'll come back to quality at the end of the session"). Don't worry about interrupting the dominating individual as he or she is typing; interruptions are more acceptable online than face to face.

After the Session

At the end of the session, regardless of whether the group is a text-based or video group, thank the participants and let them know when they can expect to be paid (if such arrangements were made beforehand). You may wish to consider an online payment system (such as PayPal) that can transfer funds directly to users' accounts.

One of the key benefits of an online text-based focus group is that the transcript is immediately available for the moderator's review. For a video group, you should be able to record the discussion; some systems even allow for a transcript to be produced. The report written by the moderator of an online focus group should follow the same guidelines as one written for an offline focus group.

ASYNCHRONOUS GROUPS

An open-ended or asynchronous group is a somewhat different type of focus group. These types of *open-ended focus groups* can occur in a bulletin board or *discussion forum* environment, or on a social networking site such as Facebook. In this first type of group, a discussion forum is set up on a company or agency website (such as Kraft.com), and a link on the homepage directs visitors to the discussion forum so they can share their opinions on specific topics. In the second type of group, a brand asks questions and gathers opinions on its Facebook wall (e.g., http://www .facebook.com/wendys) or, alternatively, sets up a new page on Facebook for discussions on a specific topic.

These asynchronous groups share some similarities with both surveys and *closed-ended focus groups*. As with a survey, garnering responses from a wide range of people is possible; however, controlling for demographics is difficult because discussion forums tend to be open to all visitors to a website and posters can be anonymous. Also like surveys, individuals provide messages and responses to questions in the discussion forum whenever it is convenient for them, making it simple to be part of the conversations. This provides a level of convenience for researchers since not everyone who is part of the group needs to be online at the same time.

Open-ended groups are similar to closed-ended groups in that participants can react and interact with messages posted by others in the group. Visitors to a website discussion forum or a Facebook wall can reply not only to the question posted by the moderator but also to comments from others visiting the site. Often, the participants in the discussion forum form a community of like-minded individuals who share ideas and opinions on all manner of topics, not just the topic of interest to account planners. These online communities are seen as a particular and unique strength of the Internet, as users grow to trust each other. This may allow for a more authentic discussion that can lead to real insights about brands.

Open-ended groups are unique from other methods in that topics either can be posted indefinitely or can be posted for a limited period of time (some types of online sites allow the researcher to "close" a discussion, while other sites require you to download the discussion and then delete its presence). The longer a topic is posted, the more opinions can be heard, but at some point, a judgment call should be made in terms of whether posts have reached redundancy. Deciding how long a discussion can be active is difficult. Some forums are more active, and one question could generate dozens of responses in less than a day. Other sites are less active, so the activity level of the specific forum should be assessed if timely data is needed. For example, if only a few posts are contributed every day, a question might need to be posted for several weeks in order to get rich data.

New questions can be added frequently, and the direction of the discussion can evolve based not only on what the account planner wishes to discuss but also on what the participants wish to discuss. In some respects, an open-ended group creates a space where visitors can help shape their own community with the assistance of the moderator. Open-ended groups create ongoing dialogues with participants that can provide rich information about perceptions of brands and advertising. On Facebook, for example, individuals can be invited to upload videos and photographs of themselves and their friends using the brand so account planners can better understand the real usage of products and services. One conversation on the Wendy's Frosty Facebook site, for example, asked how people most enjoyed a Frosty. People talked about adding coffee to give their Frosty a punch and even dipping french fries in it. These ideas resonated with many visiting the site, and such insights might appear someday in a commercial for the Frosty.

Preplanning

The planning for an open-ended group is somewhat different from that for a closed-ended group because the questions tend to be posted for long periods of time. Because a moderator is not constantly present, discussions can take on lives of their own. Therefore, agency and client personnel should discuss specific decisions and rules before establishing the forum.

Overall Purpose

First, the overall purpose of the research should be decided. Will the forum be a place where any and all discussions about the brand can occur, or will it be focused on a specific topic? For example, Procter & Gamble (P&G) has several different types of discussion forums on its website. Individuals can post short comments about any P&G product or join longer discussions where they interact with other visitors about specific P&G products. Establishing more focused discussion areas may help create a community of interaction where individuals feel comfortable sharing their opinions. P&G, for example, recognizes that the people who want to talk about Olay may not be the same people who wish to discuss Charmin toilet paper.

At the Kraft Foods website, a discussion forum titled "Wisdom of Moms" allows visitors to share thoughts and ideas on more general topics. For example, one general topic recently featured asked visitors to share tips and ideas for starting off summer on the right foot. These postings tended to feature novel ways to use different Kraft products that were time-saving and transportable for summer fun. These ideas could then be used in promotions, recipes, and other communications. At both sites, visitors are told that any comments become the property of the website sponsor (i.e., either P&G or Kraft). Links to the company's privacy policies also are clearly marked; thus, visitors can understand their legal rights regarding discussion forum participation.

Role of the Moderator

The account planner could serve as the moderator for the open-ended group, or another designated individual could take on the moderator function. Regardless, the role of the moderator should be clearly defined. The moderator should encourage and respond to postings so visitors can see that their comments are appreciated and valued. Beyond that, you must decide to what degree the moderator should monitor the postings on the forum. On Facebook, the moderator is able to bring interesting posts and comments to the forefront of the discussion.

Given that participants can post a message to the discussion board anytime, discussions not germane to the client can begin and flourish. Generally, these are termed *off-topic* discussions and evolve as participants become comfortable with the discussion forum and with one another. They signify that an online community is forming; however, they do take up bandwidth and may draw attention away from the topics that are important to you.

Establishing Policy

The anonymous nature of open-ended groups may allow individuals to participate who are not interested in the discussion but merely wish to stir up conflicts, evoke anger, and disrupt the harmony of the discussion forum. Online, these individuals are known as *trolls*. Trolls may post messages that call participants and/or their postings stupid, may post derogatory or obscene messages, and in general may try to create a negative environment on the discussion forum. Trolls usually go away if ignored. However, given the potential for such postings on your discussion forum, it is best to develop a policy upfront about deleting inappropriate messages and let posters know about the policy.

It is probably better to err on the side of hosting more off-topic information than getting a reputation for the discussion forum being so heavily moderated that a variety of opinions are not getting posted. You should, however, clearly indicate on the discussion forum (perhaps in a discussion forum procedures topic) the types of messages that will not be tolerated (e.g., those containing obscenities, hate messages, etc.). The moderator can then delete these posts. Also, be sure to put a message on the site that anything posted to the site belongs to the company and will be used for research purposes. Such a message could read,

> This is a moderated area. All messages posted to this board become the property of [client's name] and will be used only for research purposes. Use of the board is a privilege, not a right. Excessive foul language and/or vengeful or hateful posts will not be tolerated.

You should also have a client participation policy on the discussion forum. Clients should be involved, yet they should be discouraged from getting into arguments with participants in the discussion forum. Communication with the moderator regarding the postings is important and can help steer the forum discussion to areas that are of interest to all parties.

The Actual Session

In general, there isn't a formal announcement that the session has begun in an online forum. A forum is generally already active, and therefore, the account planner decides how often new topics will be posted. For example, you could post a topic of the day or a topic of the week so visitors will know there will always be something new to talk about. After a question or topic has run its course, the discussion can be closed so the discussion forum will not become too cluttered. Understand your target audience, and be sure you write to the reading level of the people who will be visiting and participating at your site.

In an open-ended session, the moderator should feel free to respond to other people's posts, not only to encourage participation (e.g., "What an interesting idea! What does everyone else think about that?") but also to probe for additional information (e.g., "Can you explain a bit more about that idea?"). Questions or discussion topics can be posted quickly, easily, and inexpensively, and frequent updates to questions will encourage participants to continually check back with the site. The moderator should plan to check the discussion forum at least twice a day. For busy forums, multiple moderators may be needed.

In some ways, the moderator has more control over the open-ended experience than can be provided during a closed-ended session because the moderator can provide specific questions for discussion, along with more in-depth background material on issues related to the topic. Visitors can access additional information via links, and participants can develop a relatively deep level of understanding of a topic. In addition, the moderator can have more control because it is difficult for an individual to dominate a message forum. Moderating the discussion forum is fairly simple because conversations do not require immediate intervention on the part of a moderator.

There are obvious trade-offs, however, in that there is less control over issues such as timing and quality of postings because it is impossible to know when people will be visiting and responding to the discussion forum. Even with a twice-a-day check of the discussion forum, an off-topic discussion may start and take over the forum before the moderator has a chance to pull the discussion back to the original topic. A disgruntled customer could also post a comment that has the potential to hurt the brand image. It is important to recognize that these conversations are just as valuable as positive conversations about the brand and to use such conversations to correct problems and provide positive brand messages at the same time.

As with closed-ended, text-based focus groups, you will lose visual cues from the individuals who are responding to the discussion forum. You cannot read their facial expressions or sense when they are being sincere or sarcastic. Thus, you may misinterpret some statements, and others participating in the discussion forum also may misinterpret them. The risk is that a misinterpretation could escalate into a conflict that is not noticed by the moderator until after some time has passed. This may result in participants developing negative feelings about the discussion forum and perhaps wishing not to return.

After the Session

As previously mentioned, consider establishing a cutoff time for each topic (e.g., every 4 to 6 weeks), although the planner should analyze data as postings occur and not wait until the cutoff time to begin analysis. However, flexibility for the cutoff date is essential: If a topic is "hot," you might think about letting it run for a few more days or a week. Similarly, if no one is responding to a topic, you may wish to delete it from the discussion forum in order to avoid a cluttered appearance. The account planner/moderator should determine the frequency of reviewing and updating the clients on the discussion forum postings. Again, this may change based on the frequency of postings and how involved the discussion becomes.

If participants register to enter a forum site, be sure to ask them if they would like to receive e-mails from you in the future. Send e-mails periodically (say, once a month or so) to those who *opt in*, reminding them to check the discussion forum and continue participating in the dialogue. Do not send them such messages too often, though, or you may be considered a spammer. Facebook also allows brands to send messages to individuals who "like" their pages, inviting them to visit the page and participate in discussions.

As with a closed-ended focus group, the transcript will be available immediately for evaluation. It can be evaluated similarly to an offline group's transcript.

DEPTH INTERVIEWING

The final type of online qualitative research involves conducting depth interviews. These can be done via text in an online chat room or using the Facebook chat feature, through e-mails, via texting on a smartphone, or with multimedia via a service such as Skype. As such, depth interviewing can be synchronous (using chat rooms or Skype) or asynchronous (using e-mail).

Online depth interviewing has many advantages. Like online focus groups, location is not an issue, so a broader range of people may agree to participate. For example, busy executives may be more willing to commit to an online interview than to other types of interviews. Online interviewing often allows for direct contact with individuals, thus avoiding secretaries, public relations departments, and the like. In addition, conflicting time zones and schedules are avoided; it is possible to interview individuals around the world, day and night (Young, Persichitte, & Tharp, 1998). Asking follow-up questions and receiving clarification on answers becomes fairly simple.

The lack of the interviewer's physical presence may also be a benefit in some situations. For example, asking questions about appearances and physical characteristics may be easier in an e-mail situation, where the participant does not have to look at the interviewer or feel that the interviewer is looking for a certain response. In this way, biases may be minimized.

Online interviews come with a few drawbacks. They may not allow the interviewer to get a good sense of the person being interviewed due to a lack of physical interaction and may limit the free flow of information back and forth, give and take, and serendipitous digressions. With asynchronous methods such as e-mail interviewing, the interviewee having the luxury of composing an answer (as opposed to giving an off-the-cuff answer) may take some of the spontaneity away from the response, but it also allows the interviewee to craft a thoughtful response to your question, regardless of the complexity.

Online interviews are not appropriate in situations where understanding an individual's emotions is important; discussing a tragedy, say, or a deeply personal issue would not work well in an e-mail environment. Topics that are more impersonal may work better for online interviews.

E-mail has become a fairly standard way of communicating for many people, and it may seem more traditional and comfortable for them than participating in a chat room or an online focus group. While text messaging may have replaced e-mail for certain demographic groups (such as young adults), e-mail is still used almost universally and allows for longer responses. Newer technologies such as Skype allow for the choice of text or video interviews and are a strong option as long as both parties are familiar with the technology. With these technologies, you also do not have to wait for the respondent to answer the e-mail in order to get your information. To interact with younger consumers, you may consider texting via a smartphone. The challenge with this technology is getting the "depth" in the depth interview, as phone texts tend to be short and snappy and may lack the important insights a planner needs.

Preplanning

As with an in-person interview, the majority of the preplanning time will be devoted to developing the questions. It is recommended that no more than 10 questions be included in the initial interview message; if necessary, you can send follow-up messages to probe or gather additional information from the individuals. The following are some tips for interview questions:

- Questions should, of course, be open-ended; be sure questions can't be answered with a simple "yes" or "no." The better the opportunity for people to say what is on their minds and talk about themselves, the better the responses will be.
- Questions should be clear, uncomplicated, and as short as possible. Start with a straightforward, easy question, and then probe attitudes and feelings.
- Number each question (and leave space for a reply in an e-mail interview).
- Be sure your final question allows interviewees to provide any additional comments on the topic that they wish.
- If you plan to use images in your interview, be sure to confirm that the participant can access them.

The Actual Interview

You are about to press the "send mail" key or click the "chat now" button on Skype. However, before you send the message or initiate the video discussion, you should be sure that, in addition to the questions, some specific information is ready to be shared with your participant.

If using e-mail, you should provide instructions on how the answers should be physically entered—either by typing an answer underneath each question or by labeling each answer with the appropriate question number. You should be sure to remind your participants of the date you need their answers returned to you and to thank them for taking the time to answer your questions. Also, advise them that you will likely be following up with them within a set period of time (say, within 24 hours of receiving the response e-mail) to ask for clarification or more information on specific topics. In that way, the participants will be expecting your follow-up and, it is hoped, will respond promptly to any additional questions you have. If you haven't received a return e-mail with the questions answered by your specified date, send a short e-mail message to the laggards reminding them of the interview and requesting that they respond at their earliest convenience. Offer to answer any questions or concerns they have either via e-mail or telephone. Also, offer to send another copy of the questions to them, in case they cannot easily access the initial e-mail. When you do receive a response, be sure to send a thank-you e-mail in return.

For a Skype interview, remind participants that you are either keeping a transcript of the text chat or recording the interview to use later. Also, ask if there is a preferred way to deal with any follow-up questions. With any type of follow-up, be timely sending the follow-up questions and include specific text from the answers you wish participants to elaborate on in case they didn't save a copy of their original responses. Try to limit the follow-up questions to five or fewer; with more, participants may feel they are being asked to participate in yet another interview that is beyond their original commitment, and they may not be as forthcoming with their answers.

One benefit of the e-mail or texted Skype is that the transcript is immediately available for analysis. Analysis should proceed as responses are returned to you and should be conducted using the same analysis techniques described earlier in this book. As with all qualitative interviews, you should allow the participant to see the transcript and make any revisions. This transcript can be sent via e-mail as a file attachment. Provide a specific time by which you would like the participants to return their comments regarding the interview.

Online Recruitment

There are numerous ways to recruit for online focus groups and interviews: for example, online banner ads, links at websites, and notices in e-mails, as well as traditional ways such as the telephone (Collins, 2000). Services such as DoubleClick provide network advertising possibilities in the form of banner advertisements for online advertisers. This means you would create a banner ad soliciting participation in the research study and provide DoubleClick with a description of the type of person you wish to recruit (from a demographic perspective). The banner would then be rotated across the thousands of webpages that are part of the DoubleClick network and meet your demographic requirements. Potential participants would click on the banner ad and complete an application form signaling their desire to participate in the group. The application form serves as a screening tool to identify the best possible participants for the focus group; specific questions on product usage and attitudes should be provided on the form. The selected participants would then be asked to confirm these answers before the start of the group as a way to make sure that the person who replied is the person who is attending the group.

Once the applications are received, the account planner can review the applicants and select participants. With this type of recruitment method, it is possible to receive thousands of completed application forms, many of which may be bogus. Sorting through the thousands of replies takes a long time. Invitations including the date and time of the group can be sent by e-mail, and applicants can respond as to whether they will attend Individuals recruited in this method generally have low "show-up" rates: a study of show-up rates by the trade publication *PR News* recommended that 20 confirmations are needed to generate a group of 10 individuals ("Securing Attendance," 2000).

New recruitment methods appear to be better techniques for finding possible participants. For example, one quick way is to post a message on your own or your company's Facebook wall or to send a tweet to your Twitter network looking for participants—a message such as, "We're looking for kayakers to help us understand what they love about the outdoors. If you want to share with us, send us your contact information." Interested people can contact you directly via the social network. The other benefit to social networking is that individuals who may not be appropriate for your research can share your request with people they know who are appropriate for the research. Therefore, you can use the power of word of mouth to recruit for your study.

Additionally, telephone recruitment has been found to obtain a better commitment and participation rate than other methods ("Securing Attendance," 2000). As with traditional groups, a list of possible participants can be purchased from a supplier with whom you already have an established relationship. Individuals can then be contacted to assess whether they are appropriate for and interested in participating in the specific group. In addition, the recruiter should assess whether the individuals have the technical skills (i.e., ability to access the Internet) and resources (e.g., a home computer with modem) necessary to participate in the online group. Because many of the individuals contacted are likely to be unfamiliar with the concept of an online focus group, the recruiter contacting the prospects can explain how the online focus group works and answer any questions individuals may have about the process. Bonding between recruiter and participant may help increase the chances that the individual recruited will actually show up for the focus group. A *PR News* study indicated that participants prescreened by telephone have the highest show-up rate at 90% ("Securing Attendance," 2000).

Another possible recruitment channel is through lists of the client company's own consumers. These lists may be obtained through the company's paper records or through e-mail registration at the company's website. Persons who are currently involved with a company's products or services may feel a greater commitment to participate; their show-up rates, according to *PR News,* are about 70% ("Securing Attendance," 2000). Of course, the limitation of this type of group is that nonusers and perhaps users of competitive products will not be included in the group.

It is also possible to purchase targeted lists of e-mail addresses for individuals who match your demographic requirements. This procedure is similar to purchasing lists of telephone numbers. This method warrants several cautions. First, many of these e-mail lists are collected in ways that may violate some consumers' perceptions of privacy. For example, *list brokers* may collect names and e-mail addresses of individuals who participate in news groups or who post their e-mail addresses on their websites. In these cases, individuals receiving unsolicited e-mail to participate in online focus groups may consider the e-mail to be *spam* and may not appreciate receiving it from you. Therefore, it is important to find a list comprising individuals who opted to be on the list—that is, they gave their permission. It is important to mention that the show-up rate for persons on such lists is fairly low: only about 50% ("Securing Attendance," 2000).

Ethical Considerations

Given the proliferation of chat rooms online, you may be tempted to forgo any type of recruiting and visit an already-existing chat room to conduct your research. For example, a PBS (2000) documentary showed researchers visiting teen chat rooms and, posing as teens, asking opinions about products and services. Many believe that this is a violation of research ethics because the researcher is pretending to be someone he is not in order to collect information. In addition, the individuals providing the information have not given their informed consent and are unaware that they are participating in a research project. This brings to mind an old *New Yorker* cartoon: "On the Internet, no one knows you're a dog" (Steiner, 1993). If you're pretending to be a teen in a chat room to conduct research, how do you know the others in the teen chat room aren't bored 30-year-olds?

Researchers conducting research online should also pay extra attention to standards of informed consent and participation. You should always make sure participants understand that they are participating in a research project and be upfront with them about how the information will be used. A quick sentence at the start of any synchronous conversation can take care of this. However, this can be challenging in an open-ended forum, where the population is constantly in flux. In this case, if research is conducted at a client forum or at a site owned by someone other than the researchers,

researchers are advised to obtain permission from forum owners and moderators, which may be a good substitute for individual consent.

What if you want to collect data from a community you are already a member of? In this situation, each individual must examine whether involvement in the community will affect how he or she performs the task of a researcher. In these cases, having a research partner may be highly useful, as you can rely on someone who may have a greater level of objectivity to help you in your work.

This brings us to a discussion of a forum where it is likely you're a member: Facebook (and other social networking sites, such as Twitter and MySpace). We've reviewed ways to use Facebook for conducting research, and as it is possible to ask questions on a brand's Facebook wall and get people to answer quickly, you are likely to get a lot of responses that you can use. When people choose to "like" your brand and participate in conversations, they are choosing to be involved in a public discussion. Even so, it does not hurt to remind people that the information they're providing can be used by the brand. What becomes more problematic is considering whether to analyze information that people already have posted on someone else's Facebook wall: For example, an account planner for Wendy's could visit the Facebook page for a competitive brand and see what people like (and don't like) about that competitor and use that information for practical recommendations. This information is often interesting to read and certainly represents the "voice" of certain consumers, but keep in mind that these people are participating because they have chosen to connect with a brand and not because they chose to be used as research subjects. They are also likely to be advocates for a brand rather than having a neutral response to a brand or subject; that is merely the nature of a social network. Needless to say, informed consent is often impossible, and it is difficult to determine demographic information of respondents. Therefore, we recommend that social media be only one part of a qualitative research study and that principles of triangulation be implemented whenever social media information is used.

Keep in mind client confidentiality as well. Testing commercials or gathering opinions on new products in a public forum could expose your clients' ideas to competitors, even if you try to put some privacy controls in place.

SUMMARY

The Internet provides new ways for account planners to connect with and learn about all types of consumers. Research can be conducted online through closed-ended focus groups (via a chat room), open-ended focus groups (via a discussion forum), and depth interviews (via e-mail). Although online consumer research might never fully replace talking with and observing consumers in their natural settings, the Internet can allow you to contact hard-to-reach individuals and engage them in the research process. Certain topics, especially those involving technology, also are appropriate for online research.

If you decide to conduct qualitative research on the Internet, you should be comfortable with online communication and recognize that traditional methods cannot be replicated in the online environment. Communication must be somewhat more explicit to make up for the lack of visual and audio cues that accompany in-person research. As with all research, upfront preparation is key to ensure that online research is successful.

In the next chapter, we shift our focus to an examination of the creative brief. The creative brief is probably the most important document that you as the account planner will develop. You've spent weeks observing, talking to, and understanding consumers and their motivations; you now have the opportunity to bring this information to life for the creative team. The creative brief is the way you do that.

KEY TERMS

asynchronous group: a group in which conversations happen sporadically over an undefined period of time.

chat room: Internet site where "real-time" interaction among multiple individuals occurs.

closed-ended focus group: Small group of people brought together in a chat room format at a specific time to answer questions posed by a moderator; a type of synchronous conversation.

discussion forum: Internet site where individuals can post messages regarding specified topics; a type of open-ended focus group.

list broker: Entity selling individual e-mail addresses.

off-topic: Posts on a discussion forum that are not germane to the specified topic of discussion.

open-ended focus group: Online discussion forum where an unlimited number of participants can respond to questions posed by a moderator; a type of asynchronous conversation.

opt in: Process by which individuals agree to receive unsolicited e-mail.

spam: Unsolicited commercial e-mail; e-mail not requested by an individual.

synchronous group: a group in which conversation happens at a specific time.

troll: Individual attempting to disrupt discussions in open-ended focus groups.

EXERCISES

1.   Set up a Facebook page for a class research project. You may wish to investigate attitudes toward a client, about a topic of interest to your class or your department, or for an on-campus group. For example, you can ask for opinions about parking on campus and try to find solutions to improve parking. Develop a plan for attracting students to the Facebook page, post questions, and monitor the discussion. Report your results to the class.

2.   Recruit several friends to participate in an e-mail interview about their favorite restaurants in your community. Prepare a series of questions, conduct the interviews via e-mail, and identify patterns in the data. You may want to ask questions such as, Tell me why this is your favorite restaurant. What makes this restaurant different from other restaurants? How do you feel when you're at this restaurant? Then repeat the exercise conducting the interviews in real time over Skype. Compare the data you get from both methods. Are the findings similar or different? Assess your own reactions to data collection in two different modes; which did you prefer and why?

RELATED READING

Jones, S. (1999). *Doing Internet research: Critical issues and methods for examining the Net*. Thousand Oaks, CA: Sage.

Mann, C., & Stewart, F. (2000). *Internet communication and qualitative research: A handbook for researching online*. Thousand Oaks, CA: Sage.

Turkle, S. (1995). *Life on the screen: Identity in the age of the Internet*. London, England: Simon & Schuster.

7

Using Research to Inspire Great Creative Work

WRITING AND PRESENTING THE CREATIVE BRIEF

The best research in the world will have no impact if the researcher cannot first find insights from the results and then find ways to inspire others to do better work based on the research. Account planners in an advertising agency and the market researchers and analysts at other types of firms embrace these two roles, and the previous chapters have suggested ways to analyze the research in order to find insights. However, knowing how to share these insights with others is also important: The way you inform others is key. This involves several skills, including distilling the information into a manageable and inspirational form and communicating the information to the creative team in a way that best stimulates creative development.

The focus of this chapter is how to present research to other people, particularly those responsible for message creation. We focus on the creative brief. Note that we use the term *creative brief*, not creative strategy or creative platform, despite the fact that you also come across the latter two terms often. We think of the creative brief in a literal way. The word *brief* means concise or free of superfluous detail. That's what your creative brief should be: the crux of all your investigations into clients' products, services, and ideas and the reactions of consumers and other stakeholders distilled into key information and insights that will inspire great work from others.

Jon Steel (1998), a renowned advertising account planner, described the creative brief as the bridge between strategic thinking and advertising; however, creative briefs can be used to inspire any type of persuasive message. Briefs are written not only for advertising campaigns but for websites, logos, packaging, and for company spokespeople being interviewed by the media. The creative brief sets the boundaries within which the art director, copywriter, creative director, and others involved in message creation can do what they do best: create effective and memorable advertising. Similarly, Lisa Fortini-Campbell (1992) has described the creative brief as the document that "introduces the creative department to the person they'll be talking to." In that way, the creative brief is "an advertisement to influence the creative team" (Steel, 1998, p. 149).

Because the creative brief begins a dialogue among researchers and message developers at the start of the creative process, the process of sharing the creative brief with the creative team is as important as the content of the creative brief itself. We begin this chapter with a discussion of the account planner's role in the advertising agency. Then we discuss why agencies develop creative briefs, describe what elements account planners commonly use in creative briefs, and provide tips on the language appropriate for the creative brief. This chapter also discusses how the creative brief is shared with the team—a meeting known as the *creative briefing*—and provides guidelines for this important meeting.

THE ROLE OF THE ACCOUNT PLANNER

Account planners are found in advertising agencies in the United States and the United Kingdom, as well as throughout the world (Patwardhan, Patwardhan, & Vasavada-Oza, 2009). Account planning captures the concept that research is more than statistics; it recognizes the "complexity of humans and their emotional attachment to products and that this understanding can be translated into effective campaigns extending far beyond agencies" (Morrison & Haley, 2006). Account planners generate strategic insights that contribute to strategy development, creative development, and campaign evaluation. Additionally, they serve as liaisons between the creative team and the account management team, and between the creative team and consumers, providing the "voice of the customer" to discussions (Morrison & Haley, 2003).

Account planning suggests solutions not only to advertising problems but to broader business problems as well. Boyko (1999) suggested that insights from account planning can inform media planning, promotions, packaging, and other types of marketing decisions. Morrison and Haley (2006) confirmed this in their study of account planners. The researchers found that planners are most involved in creative strategy development research and articulation and in evaluating tactics. Planners are involved to a lesser degree in public relations and sales promotion strategy development but generally desire an increased level of involvement in these areas.

Regardless of the type of message, then, the planner's job is to provide some degree of "discipline to the creative process." This discipline is demonstrated by the creative brief.

THE ROLE OF THE CREATIVE BRIEF

The creative brief is a communications tool. As noted earlier, the account planner uses the creative brief to begin a dialogue with the creative team regarding the advertising to be developed. The relationship between account planners and the creative team is equal, and one group (the account planner) is not giving orders or instructions to another group (the creative team). Therefore, the development of the creative brief and its presentation to the creative team reflects peer-to-peer communication that is persuasive and enlightening but not dictatorial.

Before we delve into writing a creative brief, it's important to note that different agencies approach the creative brief in different ways. We are working on the assumption that the actual creative brief will be in written format and presented to the creative team.

In some agencies, however, the creative brief is delivered in memo form to the creative team and no briefing is held. Conversely, other agencies do not allow written creative briefs, and the creative briefing is the only tool by which information is shared. The norm, however, appears to be that agencies use both a written creative brief and a creative briefing. In many agencies, the individual responsible for the creative brief is the account planner, although it may be the account executive or the planner and account executive working as a team. From this point on, we assume that the account planner is the author of the creative brief.

You may ask, "If a brief is supposed to begin a dialogue with the creative team, then why do I need to put it in writing?" That's a good question and one that begs us to examine the purposes of a creative brief. The creative brief begins the dialogue between the customer for the brand (represented by the planner) and the creative team to set the boundaries within which the advertising will be developed. It serves several other purposes, too.

- Creative briefs are documents of how advertising messages are developed. Both agency and client personnel can review several years of creative briefs that can illustrate the development of any particular brand.
- Creative briefs are a point of agreement among everyone involved in the advertising, at both the agency and the client organization. Clients will be asked to approve the creative brief, thereby indicating their agreement with its strategic direction. This can be especially beneficial if client personnel change during the course of campaign development. The client-approved creative brief is, in essence, a contract that indicates to clients what the advertising will communicate, and it may mitigate potential conflicts during a personnel change.
- Creative briefs are a reference point for creative teams in that they can continuously refer to them to keep on track as they develop the advertising.
- Creative briefs allow the agency and client account teams to develop a somewhat objective evaluation of the advertising, because the communication achieved through the advertising can be compared to the communication goals set out in the creative brief.

Creative teams see the creative brief's value as a representation of an account planner's ability to synthesize volumes of research and help them begin the creative strategy process by bringing the marketing situation (the problem and the solution) to life. Kover and Goldberg (1995) interviewed creative teams in Detroit and New York and found that, when creating advertising, copywriters and art directors often engage in one-on-one conversations with an internalized targeted consumer. As part of that process, they accept and welcome "the creative brief and other consumer-based sources of information to help them flesh out the target person" (p. 60). This finding was confirmed in a survey of creative officers in many of the top U.S. agencies (Reid, King, & DeLorme, 1998) and in a study of advertising personnel in India. In this latter study, a participant articulated the value of planning for the "softer" issues that planners bring to the table: the understanding of cultures and relationships that affects how consumers interact with brands. Account planning, in this case, was described as a combination of both logic and magic (Patwardhan et al., 2009).

Because the creative brief is the starting point for the development of the creative execution, revisions to the creative brief will likely be necessary as the account planner acquires new knowledge about consumers or about the environment under which the creative brief is being developed. In this sense, the brief should be viewed as a dynamic and evolving document. For example, during the creative briefing, the creative team may offer additional insights about the brand that they learned from working on other accounts. These would be incorporated into a revision of the creative brief. If a competitive brand begins a campaign that uses elements similar to your brand's creative brief, then the account planner may reevaluate and rewrite the creative brief given the changes in the advertising environment.

Though the brief may evolve during the development of the advertising, it is important for one individual to be the main author and "keeper" of the creative brief. One reason this is important is that the creative brief must commit to a point of view, and having a single person in charge of the creative brief best ensures this commitment. The author must also be able to defend the creative brief and its point of view to others. A single author will understand the complete thought process that went into writing the creative brief and will be best able to defend and "sell" it.

Writing the actual creative brief is a process that takes time; it is best not to try to hammer it out whenever you have a free half hour. The process of writing a creative brief takes a great deal of analysis and reflection by the account planner. The account planner should begin with a clear idea of what the client and the agency want the advertising to achieve. This advertising goal may be in terms of sales, impressions, attitudes, or awareness, or some combination of these, and may relate specifically to the goals set out in the client's marketing plan. The account planner must also think about the information that needs to be included in the message and the information that should be avoided. Most important, the account planner must review the accumulated data about the brand, the target audience, and the market in order to determine which of the key insights derived from the research is most likely to resonate with the target audience. The main insight distilled from all the information gathered through the research process becomes the essence of the account planner's point of view.

Obviously, this key insight is the focal point of the creative brief (Fortini-Campbell, 1992). The account planner needs to have an internal dialogue regarding the various insights derived from the research, gleaned from a close consideration of the various themes that occurred across the stories heard from the various respondents. Then the planner should undertake an examination of the various benefits and detriments of using each of these themes as the key insight to the brand: Why might each theme resonate with the consumer? What might potential backlashes be? The planner may also seek opinions from others involved in the process, such as the creative team and the account people, as well as from other planners who may have additional ideas about the advertising challenge facing the brand. Brainstorming and discussing the various pros and cons of different strategic alternatives is a good way to distill many ideas into the single most important thought that will motivate consumers to take the action that will meet the communication goals. Once the account planner intrinsically believes that the key insight has been found and has the research to back up the relevance of that insight, he or she can turn to the actual crafting of the creative brief.

THE BASICS OF THE CREATIVE BRIEF

Many agencies have their own formats and/or formulas for what goes into a creative brief, as you will notice in the examples provided in this chapter. While the actual formats and terminology may be different, all creative briefs tend to encompass a similar set of information.

Objective or Statement of Purpose

In this first section, account planners address questions such as, Why are we advertising? What is the problem that advertising can solve? How will the client benefit? How will consumers benefit? The *objective* will be closely related to the marketing goals established by the client in the marketing plan (Roman & Maas, 1992). If there are several levels of marketing goals, you will need to prioritize them carefully and assess which are best addressed through advertising. John Furgurson (2000) suggests that you address no more than two marketing objectives in the brief; otherwise, the message will be diluted, and you may set your brand up for failure.

Having a clear communications objective related to the marketing objective provides the ability to measure the success of the campaign once it is completed. Note in the creative brief for the bank (Table 7.1) that the objective is to build credibility for the bank while at the same time increasing awareness of its investment services. This is a communications objective that can be measured at the end of the campaign and is distinct from a marketing objective such as "sign up 10,000 new investment clients in the first year."

Tied into the objective might be some additional background about the brand or a specific articulation of the problem that must be solved. In some briefs, this problem is articulated in the form of the "consumer's current response"—that is, what the consumer is likely to say today when asked about the client. Often, these responses are direct quotes gathered from qualitative research and strongly suggest what issues need to be overcome (see the challenges articulated in the bank brief in Table 7.1, for example).

TABLE 7.1 Creative Brief for Introduce a New Financial Service (Investment Services) of an Existing Firm (The Bank)

Objective	To build the credibility of The Bank in stages, subsequently increasing awareness of The Bank's Investment Services.
Target audience	The "passive investor": that segment of the affluent market who have the knowledge to do their own investing but would rather do other things. They are confident that their investment consultant will make the best decisions concerning their portfolio.
Competition	Any type of investment service, online or offline.
What the target currently thinks	The word *bank* denotes an image of poor customer service and conservatism.
What we want them to think	The Bank's Investment Services is a firm that works for the clients in a revolutionary way: providing them with high returns. Period.
Single most important thought	The Bank provides straightforward investing, focusing on only one purpose of investing: making money.
Support	Investment history of consultants, dedicated consultants who respect wealth.
Suggested channels	Television and print, as well as social media, direct marketing, and word of mouth.

Note: Brief can be used for advertising creative development as well as direct marketing and public relations efforts.

Target Audience

The creative brief should focus on the consumer and present the advertising challenge from his or her perspective. This section describes the consumer from numerous perspectives: demographically, psychographically, and in terms of product/service usage and behavior. Jon Steel (1998) says the brief should contain a descriptive and emotional portrait of the consumer. Look for truths that bind different consumers together—shared meaningful aspects of their lives (Furgurson, 2000).

The target audience description should give insight into how consumers think and feel. Fortini-Campbell (1992) describes this section as the way to put the consumer at the table with all other members of the advertising team. To do this, use both demographics and psychographics, giving a broad description of the individuals that the creative will be "talking to" with advertising messages.

Competition

Both short-term and long-term competitors should be identified. For a spaghetti sauce product, for example, short-term competition might be all other jarred sauces; long-term competition might include canned tomatoes, tomato paste, packaged sauce mixes, and other bases that a cook could use to create a sauce to his or her taste. This can be done explicitly, as shown in the bank brief (Table 7.1), or implicitly, as in the peanut butter brief (Table 7.2), which indicates that any type of food used as "fuel" could be a competitor for peanut butter.

Chosen Communication

The *chosen communication* is sometimes termed the *key insight, single most important thought,* or *key promise*; it is what you hope consumers will take away from the advertising message. The insight will pull together all the research and show how it fits into the bigger context of the advertising message. The techniques described earlier in this book should help you discover the key consumer insights that will motivate consumers to purchase your brand.

TABLE 7.2   Creative Brief to Create Preference and Loyalty for an Existing Product (Peanut Butter)

Objective	To increase brand preference and ultimately loyalty among current users.
Target	Demographics: 25- to 49-year-old college-educated professionals dwelling in urban areas. Psychographics: Career-oriented, health-conscious, and practical shoppers. Care about eating healthy but don't want to spend a lot of time planning meals or shopping. Appreciate quality food but do not have the mind-set of a "foodie"; instead, they view food as fuel.
Current thought	"Peanut butter sandwiches were fun as a kid and a cheap way to eat in college."
Desired thought	"Adam's provides a healthy peanut butter for adults to indulge in."
Rationale	Audience wants to make smart purchasing choices and healthy dietary decisions.
Single most important thought	Adam's inspires the user to slow down and enjoy the peanut butter–eating experience and everything that means.

Note: Brief can be used for advertising creative methods.

Also included in this section is the *support,* or reasons why the target will believe the message focus. Support points can include both product attributes and consumer attitudes. In the vitamin brief (Table 7.3), the key insight is an emotional promise to the target, and the support consists of logical and rational facts.

TABLE 7.3 Creative Brief for Personal Communications: Vitamin A Distribution in Third-World Markets

Objective	To encourage families to bring children up to 6 years old to health centers to receive Vitamin A capsules (VAC).
Problems to overcome	Capsule distribution had been most effective on designated national immunization days, which no longer exist. Families rarely bring children to health centers if they are not sick, and there is a lack of information about the benefits of Vitamin A.
Key promise/benefit	Mothers and families will be happy and confident once they have taken their children for VAC. Mothers/families will know they are good parents who take care of their children.
Support statements	VAC protects a child from serious disease and saves lives; VAC protects a child from blindness; VAC is free and has no side effects or dangers.
Tone	Personal, emotional, parent-to-parent, reassuring, warm.

Note: Brief would be distributed to health workers addressing family groups and conducting media interviews.

Mandatory Inclusions/Exclusions

The creative team needs to know if there is any information that must or must not be included in the advertisement. Certain information is often included in the advertising for legal reasons. For example, advertising for many types of bank products must by law include specific financial disclosure information. Occasionally, the creative team may need to be reminded of industry advertising guidelines for specific product categories. For example, the beer beverage industry has a guideline that adults not be shown drinking beer in commercials.

Although the above elements are the foundation of the brief, there is other information that may or may not be included. In general, an agency-wide decision will determine whether the following elements are incorporated.

Style or Tone

Roman and Maas (1992) describe style or tone as the "projection of your product's personality." The style or tone should be directional in nature and should, again, broadly define boundaries within which the creative team can work best. Examples of appropriate language for style or tone include words such as *serious, happy, bright, magical, wholesome,* and *trendy*: the vitamin brief (Table 7.3) suggests vocal styles that would increase the persuasive aspects of the message.

Timing

Including some indication of when the advertising is planned to begin will help the creative team manage its workload. It also allows the team to capitalize on any seasonal imagery that may affect the work. Avoid informing the creative team that the advertising is needed immediately or ASAP, because these terms are ambiguous.

THE LANGUAGE OF THE CREATIVE BRIEF

The written creative brief should be both directional and inspirational. It is directional in that it should let the creative team know what is required of the advertising, in terms of advertising goals as well as specific information that must be included. Constraints on the advertising, in terms of information that must be added or avoided, are generally also included. The information presented for guidance should establish the parameters under which the creative team works, but it should not become hard-and-fast instructions. For example, look at the following two possible ways to craft the statements in a creative brief regarding required information in an advertisement. In this case, the client specified that the logo should be shown for a specific amount of time during the commercial. In most cases, this logo was shown at the end of the commercial. However, that convention was not set in stone.

> Client logo must be featured in the final 3 seconds of the television spot.

> Client logo should be visible during at least 1/10 of total commercial time.

The first example provides executional direction to the creative team. The second example sets a parameter but allows for some creativity in deciding where the 3-second logo shot is placed, which loosens the restriction on the creative team.

The directional nature of the creative brief can be enhanced if the creative brief is sharply focused and neither verbose nor ambiguous. A verbose creative brief is not only a contradiction in terms but also may allow for interpretations of the writing that perhaps the planner did not intend. An ambiguous creative brief can also lead to misinterpretation, because the creative brief has not committed to a point of view. Consider these three examples of target audience descriptions for a jar of spaghetti sauce.

> Moms with kids under 12.

> Moms with kids under 12 who probably do not prepare a lot of meals from scratch but generally use a variety of packaged goods as the basis for their meals. These moms may be users of products such as jarred spaghetti sauce and packaged dinners, and they also may be users of foods purchased from the deli counter of their grocery store. They are also busy and highly involved in the lives of their children.

> Moms who consider themselves creative and somewhat adventurous in the kitchen but need to balance their creativity with the demands of the picky eaters in the family.

After reading the first example, do you have an image of the consumer in your mind? Neither do we. The first example provides nebulous information about the target consumer to the creative team. The second example provides quite a bit of information but no real inspiration: The description is likely to fit virtually every mom with kids under 12 in the United States. This example is verbose and provides several options for the creative team to peruse. Though this may be somewhat liberating for the creative team, it is possible that the advertising will not be focused or relevant to the target audience. The third example creates a much more vivid picture for everyone reading the creative brief. It describes what is unique and different about the moms who are in the target compared with the other moms who may fit the profile demographically (i.e., have kids under 12) but not psychographically (i.e., do not consider themselves adventurous).

The creative brief should be inspirational in that it encourages the creative team to strive to create the best advertising possible. To be inspirational, the creative brief should be imaginative, stimulating, and involving. To use an artistic metaphor, the creative brief should be the palette of paints presented to the artist (the creative team) for the creation of a masterpiece. Take, for example, two different ways to describe consumer insights regarding jarred spaghetti sauce.

> Creative cooks know that jarred spaghetti sauce does not have to be boring. Other ingredients can be added to spice it up; use your imagination to make the sauce that is most appealing for you and your family.

> Jarred spaghetti sauce is just the start. What happens next is up to the cook!

The first example is unexciting. It provides direction but does not necessarily inspire the creative team. The second example presents a more vivid description of the insight and can help the creative team focus its energy into the optimal message for the advertisement. Try to write as visually as you can; see if your words sound like words consumers in your target would say or react to.

ASSESSING THE CREATIVE BRIEF

Once the creative brief is drafted—but before it is presented to the creative team—the planner should check it over, asking the following questions.

Is the Creative Brief Logical and Consistent?

The elements of the creative brief should fit together logically in that each piece of information builds on the information previously provided. Another way to answer this question is to ask if the creative brief is committed to a point of view. If it is, then all the elements of the creative brief should work together to support that point of view.

Does the Creative Brief Provide Information That Is New and Insightful?

If the creative brief is just a rehashing of the information the creative team already knows and has used to create previous campaigns, there will be little to excite and inspire them. The account planner should always be on the lookout for new insight to give the creative team a fresh way of looking at and thinking about the consumer, thereby developing a new perspective among the team members.

Is the Creative Brief Believable and Supportable?

Not only must the creative brief be logical and insightful, it also must be believable; that is, the account planner must be able to solicit agreement among all members of the team that the approach is inherently "right" for reaching the target audience. Providing backup research results is one way to support the creative brief and persuade members of the team that the approach is inherently right.

Is the Creative Brief Clear and Simple?

A team member reading the creative brief should be able to recount one or two key ideas that encompass its essence, framed in the words of the consumer. The creative brief should be written in language that the consumer would use. Limiting the creative brief to a single page is one way to ensure that it is clear and simple. The single-page format forces the planner to remain constantly focused on the most important insights and to weed out all extraneous information. Although this may seem like an arbitrary cutoff point for such an important document, Roman and Maas (1992) argue that if you can't fit the information onto one page, the chances of getting it all into a 30-second commercial are slight.

Is This the Best Way to Introduce the Consumer to This Specific Creative Team?

Finally, the planner should reflect on what he or she knows about the creative team that will be working on the advertising and think about how the team will react to the creative brief. The creative team's level of familiarity with the target audience and the language the consumers speak and the team's previous involvement with the brand and the research will help determine the level of information and presentation style that will best inspire the team.

PRESENTING THE BRIEF

The original manifesto developed by the British Account Planning Group (n.d.) stated that in the advertising world, no one has a monopoly over wisdom or ideas; an agency consists of a group of people with different skills, abilities, experiences, and personalities trying hard to get the best possible advertising for their clients.

A good relationship between the account planner and the creative team (i.e., the copywriter and art director, and possibly the creative director) is based on trust and cooperation. The creative team must trust that the information contributed by the account planner is accurate and focused. Few things can ruin this relationship more than research that is perceived to be irrelevant or unnecessary. In talking with various creatives from different agencies across the United States as we prepared this book, we found one story in particular that exemplifies this point.

We asked various creatives about their relationships with planners and how they wanted research insights to be presented. One Chicago creative, whom we will refer to as RK, responded,

> It's [research] all useless! I never will forget one time when this young kid stood up in front of us to say that all the research led to one conclusion: "The number one reason

people buy ketchup is the taste." For crying out loud! You just spent $40,000 to tell me that? Give me something useful or shut up.

You wouldn't want to be on the receiving end of that tirade, would you? Such encounters with research led RK not to want anything to do with planners or research. He commented, "Creatives get paid to reach people. I know how to do that without all this research bunk." The good news is that most of the creatives we spoke with who worked in planning agencies saw value in planning, and they reported good relationships with their planners. We strongly feel that for planning to be optimally effective, the account planner, creatives, and other members of the strategy team must be willing to work synergistically to execute the strategy. To develop a good relationship with the creative team, an account planner must establish a dialogue with the team members about the research problem at hand. To develop this relationship, we recommend doing the following:

- Recognize that every creative team is different. Get to know each of the copywriters and art directors with whom you're working and understand how the team works, particularly how they like to get information. To better understand their communication style, watch them interact with other creative teams and with account managers. Find out what motivates them. Take them to lunch when you aren't working under a deadline, and learn who they are as individuals—just as you would with any consumer!
- Seek the copywriter's and art director's advice early in the process, particularly regarding strategic issues. Ask them about their experiences with other clients. What did they perceive as problems and benefits of using research in the past? This type of discussion fosters an early sense of trust.
- Share the passion that the copywriter and art director have for advertising. Advertising is their art. Recognize that no idea is a bad idea, and work with the team to create polished diamonds out of their rough ideas.
- Inspire, don't instruct. Remember, you're all part of the same team, working toward the same goal. You're not the boss of the creative team; you are a member of the team.

ENHANCING THE CREATIVE BRIEF

You may wish to enhance the brief by identifying visual and audio elements that help bring the consumer to life. This can inspire the creative team by helping them visualize the people for whom they are constructing advertising messages. If your target audience is soccer moms, for example, go out and take photographs or shoot a video of these women cheering on their teams; the video can show the creative team what the consumers wear, how they style their hair, and how they speak to their kids and to one another. If your target is teenage boys, create a playlist of music they listen to, prepare clips of the TV programs they are likely to watch, or download the websites they visit most often. All these methods are ways to bring the target audience to life for the creative team. Refer back to Chapter 3 for more examples of how to bring the research to life.

Remember that, by and large, creatives want information to be *brief* and to the point. When presenting additional information, choose wisely. Which audio quotes best communicate the targeted consumer's viewpoint? Edit these into a short audio presentation. Similarly, which visuals best communicate the essence of your targeted consumer's experience? Again, edit these into a brief videotape or develop a few oversized photos of your targeted consumers to hang in the room as your team is discussing strategy. What you do with this type of data (if anything) depends on your particular creatives. Just like the brief, this type of presentation should feed the creative process. If such input is not useful to your creatives, then these ideas will likely be a distraction. These types of enhancements to the brief also can be of assistance in selling the creative brief, your strategy, and executions to the client.

FINDING THE MOST COMPELLING WAY TO DELIVER THE STRATEGY

Qualitative research can be useful in directing the creative product in other stages of the advertising development process beyond development of the initial creative brief.

Often, a great strategy can go many different directions. The creative team's your job is to figure out the most relevant and compelling way to communicate the strategy to your target. Additional qualitative research with target consumers can help refine the strategy and direct you toward a winning executional concept for your advertising.

Consider this example. Through solid qualitative research with small-business owners, your team's planners have delivered a strategy for your client's office equipment product that says, "Client X's office equipment helps the small-business owner work smarter." Your job as a creative is to figure out how to communicate "working smarter" to your targeted small-business owner in the most motivating way. Many compelling benefits could stem from "working smarter." It might mean the small-business owner saves time at work so she can have more free time with her family. It might mean the small-business owner makes more money so she can have more luxury time to herself. Maybe personal life motivations are not the most compelling motivators for a small-business owner; perhaps "working smarter" means being more successful and growing the business, where the growth of the business is the owner's motivating factor. There are other options as well. The job of the creative is to brainstorm the many ways "working smarter" can be motivating to the small-business owner and hone in on the best way to communicate the benefits of buying the client's office equipment.

One way to help creatives make that decision is to invite target market consumers to view multiple advertising concepts. Creatives might develop five or six ads for each concept option (free time with family, more money for personal luxury, satisfaction of growing the business, etc.). Why develop more than one execution for each strategic option? If you have only one execution for each option, you might not be able to tell if the consumer is responding to the message or some specific executional element in that one example. For example, consumers may not like the illustration and just focus their attention there, not talking about the message at all (which is what you really want to hear about).

Post the various ads for each concept in groups around the room; each group of ads should represent one strategic option. As consumers are looking at the various ads, start interviewing them. Ask them what each group of ads is saying to them. Ask which, if any, seem to be more motivating to them. Probe to find out why.

Try to tease out if consumers are responding to the idea or specific executional elements in specific ads. For example, you could ask, "Within this group of ads, are there any particular ads you like more or less than the others? Why?" Insights from this type of qualitative research not only can help you refine your message but might suggest specific executional tactics you should consider or avoid in your final ads.

A FINAL CHECK

You've spent a great deal of time, energy, and money to develop a great strategy and compelling creative, but how do you know if your creative is really delivering the message you intend to deliver? Qualitative research can help here, too.

As a final check, you could ask target market members to view your finished executions. In a semistructured interview, you would want to ask them, "What is this ad saying?" Some call this a consumer "takeaway" statement (i.e., what the consumer takes away from viewing the ad). If all is working right, the consumer should be echoing the strategy you intended. If the consumer is coming away from the ad with a message different from what you intended, it's better to know that before spending dollars to place the ad in media. If the statement is different, then you need to use the interview time to explore what is leading the consumer to the message she is receiving from your ad so that you understand where the communication failure is occurring.

SUMMARY

Qualitative research can help at several stages of creative development, from strategy development to checking the final ad executions. Qualitative research can lead to the generation of the creative brief. The brief should begin the dialogue about strategy and, once the strategy is agreed on, should be the expression of that strategy. Just like research, creating a brief requires a team of equals who are willing to work together as partners in strategy creation. The creative brief is an important document. All members of your team, especially the client, need to understand it, embody it, and use it throughout the advertising creation and evaluation process. The creative brief outlines the key insight the planner discovered through research. This key insight is the focus of the brief. Qualitative research can help you refine a strategy, develop executional strategy, and ensure that you're communicating the message you intended.

Although the forms that creative briefs take often differ from agency to agency, the brief usually includes information about the following: the purpose of the advertising, the target audience, the competition, the key insight, mandatory inclusions/exclusions that relate to the advertising, the budget, the timing of the campaign, and the style or tone the planner thinks the advertising should adopt. Visual and audio elements can be used to enhance the brief and give the strategy team a better feel for the targeted consumer. The language of the brief should be descriptive and bring the consumer to life for the strategy team.

Before presenting the brief to the creative team, the planner should double-check it for consistency, logic, innovation of the insight being presented, and clarity of thinking.

In the next chapter, we offer some additional lessons learned from our experiences developing qualitative research for various advertising and marketing projects. We hope that these additional insights will save you some of the headaches we've endured when faced with sticky situations.

KEY TERMS

chosen communication: Central idea or "single most important thought" that the advertising message should convey.

creative brief: Document that inspires the creative team to produce exceptional advertising.

creative briefing: Meeting in which the account planner shares the creative brief with the creative team.

objective: Overall goals of advertising campaign.

support: Reason why the chosen communication is appropriate for the target audience and the campaign.

EXERCISES

1. We all persuade other people every day. Think of an upcoming event where you need to persuade someone: you need to get an exam moved, you need to get into a closed class, you want to try to get out of a parking ticket. Write a "creative brief" to help frame your arguments, and include the important elements discussed in this chapter.

2. Select several print advertisements from a magazine you read regularly. "Reverse engineer" the advertising strategy of the print ad; that is, see if you can identify the target audience, advertising objective, chosen communication, and tone. Were some advertisements easier to reverse engineer than others? Why might this be?

3. Select a movie or television show you've seen recently. Write a creative brief promoting the movie or show without providing the actual title. Switch briefs with a partner to see if you can determine the movie or TV show that is the focus of the brief.

RELATED READING

Boyko, R. (1999, July). *The evolution of an idea*. Paper presented at the Account Planning Conference, San Diego, CA.

Fortini-Campbell, L. (2001). *Hitting the sweet spot* (2nd ed.). Chicago, IL: Copy Workshop.

Mondroski, M. M., Reid, L. N., & Russell, J. T. (1983). Agency creative decision making: A decision systems analysis. *Journal of Current Issues and Research in Advertising, 23*, 57–69.

Morrison, M., & Haley, E. (2003). Account planners' views on how their work is and should be evaluated. *Journal of Advertising, 32*(2), 7–16.

Morrison, M., & Haley, E. (2006). The integration of account planning in U.S. advertising agencies. *Journal of Advertising Research, 46*, 124–132.

Patwardhan, P., Patwardhan, H., & Vasavada-Oza, F. (2009). Insights on account planning: A view from the Indian ad industry. *Journal of Current Issues and Research in Advertising, 31*(2), 107–119.

Philips, P. L. (2004). *Creating the perfect design brief: How to manage design for strategic advantage*. London, England: Allworth.

Roman, K., & Maas, J. (1992). *The new how to advertise*. New York, NY: St. Martin's.

Steel, J. (1998). *Truth, lies, and advertising: The art of account planning*. New York, NY: John Wiley.

8

Balancing Ideals and Real-World Constraints

This book has discussed how to use various qualitative research techniques to generate quality consumer insights. We've presented the techniques in ways that we feel optimize the richness of the information you can get from them. However, experience has taught us that the world of business often forces you to make some tough decisions. This chapter is a brief discussion of some ways to balance research ideals with real-world constraints in a manner that still will generate high-quality research findings. Specifically, we deal with issues of budget, optimal scheduling, convincing clients to allow questions that deal with context, and incorporating a client's *mandatory questions* when the questions don't seem to fit the purpose and nature of the research.

BUDGET

Qualitative research can be expensive and time-consuming. We've found that clients who are inexperienced with investing in qualitative research tend to think of it as being less expensive than quantitative research. Statements from clients such as, "But I can get a national *hard numbers* survey for less than this," can be frustrating. The answer

165

is, "Yes, sometimes you can get a national hard numbers survey for less than this." Then, the process of educating the client begins.

First, be sure your explanation includes the phrase, "Quality research is an *investment*." Then, take the client back to the goals of the study, reminding him or her why the research needs to be done in the first place. One exercise we have used with resistant clients is having them play along (if they will) with a little research project. Give them a short survey of questions on their business lives that takes about 5 minutes to complete. After they complete the survey, ask them to assess how much they think you know about what it's like to be them and work where they work. Usually, the answer is "not much." Then ask them to tell you about their work life. That will lead into a short interview. Try to ask the same number of questions that were on the survey. Then ask them which technique gives a better understanding of what life is really like for them. Of course, they'll usually say the interview is the better technique (if they don't, then give up and use a survey—you'll probably never make them happy with anything else). This little exercise is a way to remind clients why they wanted to engage in the research to begin with. Then you can present a brief comparison of the budget needed for a national quantitative study and the budget for the qualitative study at hand.

When comparing budgets, it's essential to talk about the time involved in data collection and analysis. Numerical data entry and tab houses are relatively cost- and time-efficient. Transcribing an interview verbatim, verifying the transcription, and then making sense of the pages and pages of text is time- and cost-intensive. The entire point of this exercise is to show clients that, yes, they can get a national survey for less money, but to get the type of data that will generate the insights that resonate with consumers' lives and will take their marketing efforts to the next level, they should invest in the qualitative study.

REDUNDANCY AND BUDGET CONSTRAINTS

In optimizing research findings and meeting budget constraints, one trade-off may come when dealing with the *redundancy criterion*. Recall that in ideal qualitative studies, you know you've done enough research when thematic redundancy emerges from the analysis. Listening for redundancy has budget implications. Specifically, when planning the study, it's difficult to predict how many subjects you will need to recruit to reach redundancy. How your target market is defined impacts how quickly you can reach this goal. People who are more alike than different share common experiences. If your population of interest is homogenous, then you can expect to reach redundancy fairly quickly. One methodologist suggests that with homogenous populations, redundancy may be reached in as few as eight interviews (McCracken, 1988). However, if your target market is defined broadly and is diverse, then you will likely need many more participants to reach the redundancy goal.

If you run into budget constraints when planning the research project, take a long, hard look at your target population. Can this population be more narrowly defined? Are you talking with the type of people who can give you the most useful insight? For example, recall in Chapter 3 where we talked about a recent study of college students' credit card use; we were interested in understanding how college students understood their financial prowess and how they defined and dealt with credit card trouble. We initially began the study by talking with college students of all ages. It probably isn't surprising that almost all felt they could handle their finances better than their friends could, most thought they were good at handling their credit card debt, and few worried about it. Very few felt they were in trouble. These statements ran counter to national statistics on college students' credit card debt. However, when talking with graduate students or older college students, we found terrific insights. For this study, hindsight was better. We had been talking to the wrong audience and too broad an audience. Young people in the midst of accumulating debt often cannot see the trouble they are getting into. Only when talking to seniors and graduate students did insights begin to emerge about how they woke up to their debt problems, about things they wished they had known at a younger age, and about what it would have taken to get through to them as younger students. By more narrowly defining our population and asking who could give us the best understanding of this phenomenon, we were able to greatly reduce the number of subjects (and money) needed for the project, and we got much more useful data that could feed the creative process.

Finding the Right Participants Versus Easy Participants

The above example shows the value of finding the right participants. Sometimes, though, you may be asked to find participants
quickly. Some planners have confessed to using their agency staff
(secretaries, etc.) or family members of the agency staff as an easy
way to get some ideas in a pinch. Others have said they've used
their own parents as research participants. That someone has a
close relationship with you doesn't necessarily invalidate them
as a research participant; however, there are some pitfalls to consider. If you know that person well, you may make assumptions
about what he or she means rather than asking for confirmation,
or you may avoid certain questions because you think you already
know the answer. If you do pick an "easy" participant, one whom
you know well, you will have to work to "manufacture distance"
(McCracken, 1988). That is, you'll have to work extra hard to
make someone familiar to you more novel or distant so you won't
assume too much. In other words, you have to make sure you treat
the person you know just like a person you don't know.

You also must be careful that your "easy" participants (those
easiest to recruit) come from the same lived experiences as your
target market. If they are part of your client's target group or your
research population, then great! If not, you will need to closely
think about how they might be different. It may be easier to recruit
New Yorkers if your agency is in New York City, but if your target
population is Midwestern suburbanites, will the easier New York
recruits be able to share the experience of someone living in the
Midwestern suburbs? You could end up making some incorrect
leaps of faith if you're not careful. Rather than using familiar people as research participants, perhaps a better way to use them is to
enlist their help in finding the right people you need.

OVER-RECRUITING

Another tendency you might encounter is clients who are used
to quantitative studies wanting you to over-recruit for qualitative
work. For example, it may seem logical that if you are representing
a national marketer, you must have a national sample to sufficiently

explore the lived experience of that marketer's customers. This may not be the case. Consider the example of the home-office businessperson. Home-office businesspeople work in all areas of the United States, but they share a common experience—working from home. They must deal with the same issues of technology, scheduling, the relationship between work and home life, and more, regardless of whether they're working in Los Angeles or Key West. We talked earlier in the book about realities being *context* specific. Here, the context is shared—working from home. The context isn't necessarily the city or state in which the person works. In this example, you could generate the same quality insights from looking at a variety of home businesspeople within one small, one medium, and one large market as you would if you went to the expense and logistical lengths of attempting to field the study nationally. Examine the context of the phenomenon carefully when considering participant selection.

COST-EFFECTIVE RESEARCH BASED ON CLIENT ROSTERS

Not every client will be willing to invest in the research needed to break through the message clutter. Nevertheless, planners' and agencies' jobs are on the line to produce work that moves the marketer toward his or her goals. One strategy to combat this is for agencies to examine their client rosters and develop *agency-wide research initiatives* that can serve multiple clients. Use the target markets or product categories of clients on your roster to identify commonalities around which you can develop research initiatives. Examples of such clusters may be kids, home-office workers, fast-food retailers, or purchasing agents within a specific industry. By developing a good understanding of how kids think, feel, and live, you may be able to help a variety of your clients develop communications and marketing plans that will resonate with the population—for toys, video games, fast food, clothes, school supplies, recreational equipment, and the like. Each of the aforementioned marketers needs to understand the lived realities of kids in order to understand the role their product or service plays in kids' lives. Rather than reinventing the wheel each time one of your clients approaches kids as a market, you already will be aware of the unique information the client needs and will have the basic information. This will allow you to move quickly to help the client develop a solid strategy and will give you a basis from which to develop a reputation as the "kids expert" that attracts new business.

SCHEDULING

Ideally, qualitative research follows an emergent design. Emergent designs give researchers the flexibility needed to uncover unanticipated truths and delve deeper into the participants' lived experiences. We feel that emergent design is a major strength of qualitative research. It takes time, though, and notions of emergent design don't always square with a marketer's timetable. In an age when most things should have been done yesterday, it takes effort to make sure researchers and planners have time for *reflection*. After all, the best insights often are not the first insights that come to mind.

From the start, you should talk with your account team and client about the importance of pacing a qualitative investigation. Ideally, you should build time between interviews or other participant contact to give the researchers a chance to review the encounter and adjust questions or methods for the next encounter. If multiple researchers are collecting data, then time should be allowed for the researchers to review individually and together the initiative's progress. We strongly feel it is in the best interest of all involved *not* to give instant feedback to clients after a group interview or other participant contact. Again, the best insights result from reflection.

In light of these issues, we've found it best to overestimate slightly the time it will take to field and analyze qualitative research. Finishing ahead of schedule is more pleasant than reporting delays.

USING MULTIPLE RESEARCHERS TO SAVE TIME

Account planners often hire outside research suppliers to conduct primary research, particularly on large projects. Often, planners will find themselves working with multiple researchers. Using multiple researchers to field a study has time benefits but also presents some unique considerations. Recall that in qualitative investigations the researcher is the instrument. To get a good understanding of what our participants' thoughts, feelings, and lives are like, the researchers must have the flexibility to follow participants' lines of thought, discover unanticipated issues, and modify or change the methodology in order to best capture the respondents' experiences. This feature of qualitative techniques requires well-trained researchers.

When hiring researchers/interviewers through field houses, we've learned that *interviewer-administered surveys* are often mistaken for qualitative interviews. The skill level required to read questions and record answers is not the same skill set that a good qualitative interviewer needs. When considering an outside research supplier, ask what types of qualitative studies the field house has conducted in the past. Also, see if you can ascertain what kind of training the interviewers have had. If you're not careful, you will end up with an interview in which you learn more about the interviewer than the participant, an interview with garbled and unanswerable questions (often where probes are asked in the same breath as the lead question, to the point that the participant has no chance to remember the question), and ultimately an interview that is a costly waste of time and money.

Also keep in mind that the researcher is the interpreter of the participants' experiences. The researcher should be viewed as one of the planner's *partners* in strategy development. Seeking researchers/interviewers experienced with the product category or the target market can enhance this relationship.

As you might guess from the above comments, we feel that the continuity one or a small number of researchers/interviewers can bring is a great benefit to the research initiative. If you do have to use a large and geographically diverse group of interviewers, there are some ways to help the process along.

First, prepare a good training guide that explains the marketer's situation and the goals of the research initiative. Include directions with the discussion guide or any other data collection tools that explain the type of flexibility the researchers have with the instrument. An example of a transcript or videotape that you consider to be a good interview could also be helpful. If possible, pay a visit to or conduct a conference call with the interviewers prior to data collection so you can review the goals of the study, answer questions, and preempt problems. Knowing that your instructions have been noticed and everyone is on the same page brings peace of mind. During data collection, visits or conference calls also are extremely important. Such contact can give you time to reflect along with the interviewers/researchers and adapt the method as needed to generate the data you need for discovering that key insight.

GETTING PERMISSION TO ASK THE QUESTIONS YOU NEED AND AVOIDING QUESTIONS YOU DON'T

The relationship between the planner and researcher is critical to a successful research initiative. As we mentioned earlier, this means looking at the researcher's role not as that of a supplier but, rather, as a partner. Open communication is vital. Planners and researchers need to talk through the marketer's situation in order to know what type of information that client needs. If possible, having the researcher meet directly with the client can enhance the researcher's ability to probe and provide an analysis that addresses the client's business goals.

Sometimes, in the conversation between parties, conflicts arise regarding the content of research questions/procedures. At times, the client will be resistant to asking questions of your research participants that you know you need to ask, and other times, you will be reluctant to ask certain questions the client feels are necessary. Although there is no one way to address all potential conflicts, we have found some successful strategies for dealing with certain types of question conflicts.

Clients often want the research to get to the point right away. As you recall from the chapter on interviewing, building rapport with the participant and understanding the context of that participant's life are extremely important aspects of any qualitative data collection method. Factors such as consumers' purchasing and business decisions occur within the larger context of how the consumers or businesspeople approach the world. Time is money, and asking general questions about a person's life takes time (and, therefore, money), but the information garnered during such general exploration is often where the best insights are found. We've found two examples that can explain this clearly to an account team or client.

The first example deals with developing a communications campaign to address the growing spread of HIV/AIDS among rural young adults. The previous campaigns had targeted men in urban centers; however, messages from those campaigns did not resonate with women or the rural experience. To design a campaign that better reflected the new environment, we embarked on an ethnographic study of both men and women in a Southern rural community. During the study, we found that among many lower income white males, medical facts about the spread of HIV/AIDS were being reversed. These young men would say things such as, "AIDS is the woman's fault; a woman is more likely to give HIV/AIDS to a man than a man is to a woman." At first glance, it seemed as though these men just had the wrong information— information that was putting women at risk. However, because we took the time and effort to learn more about these men's lives and how they viewed the world, these statements began to make sense (at least within their worldview).

The men making these statements had long histories of divorce in their families; some had been arrested for spousal abuse. They would make statements such as,

> The judge in town has his hand in the man's back pocket [when settling divorce cases]. All a woman has to do is cry a little and she gets everything: Man's suffering is due to Eve, she took the apple from the Devil; Adam didn't.

When placing the "facts" about HIV/AIDS transmission as understood by these young men in the context of their overall understanding of women, why these men attributed AIDS to women was evident. Strategically, this called into question whether any communication campaign could break through to these men to get them to take more responsibility for the spread of the virus. What we were up against wasn't incorrect knowledge but deeply rooted cultural understandings of the relationship between men and women.

The second example has to do with a product distributor and his relationship with his retailers. This particular distributor had been dealing with retailers that were major corporations. All the distributor's programs were set up for large retail bureaucracies; however, a fair amount of his product was sold via stores owned and operated by small-business people. Small-business retailers were particularly perplexing to the distributor, so he wanted some research. Initially, the distributor wanted the small-business retailers to evaluate a series of proposals for programs the distributor felt would enhance the sale of the product through these outlets. All these programs involved the distributor taking an active role in running the small-business owner's store. In the interviews, these program ideas were met with much resistance from the small-business owners. Had we not taken the time to understand what motivated people to start their own small business, the satisfaction they received from running the business, and the frustrations they experienced, we would not have understood why these program suggestions were met with such disdain. The general context questions revealed right away that these small-store owners liked being the "captains of their own ships." They went into business for themselves to gain control. They were tired of working for others. They achieved satisfaction from both successes and failures, because the successes and failures were their own. All the distributor's suggestions ran counter to the core motivation these small-business owners had for opening their own shops. Because we asked the context questions upfront, we could move the conversation toward understanding what type of help the business owners wanted from the distributor and in what form they wanted that help delivered. Had we not asked these questions, we would have known only that the participants didn't like our program ideas.

As we discussed in Chapter 2, asking questions that build context does pay off. You may not know how it will benefit you at first, but given that meaning arises through context, understanding context is critical.

Another area of frequent conflict is the inclusion of questions that the planner or researcher feels are inappropriate for the methods being used. If it's apparent that your client or account team is insisting on lines of questioning that don't lend themselves well to qualitative methods, there are a couple of paths you can take to limit the potential damage inappropriate questions can cause to the project.

First, explore with the account team or client other avenues for gathering the desired data. For example, in a study with a product distributor, the corporate director for the project insisted that questions about store attributes be included in one-on-one interviews with store owners—questions such as whether a store used endcap displays and how many, what square footage was allotted to what types of products, if certain products were displayed in particular ways, and so forth. The list went on and on. We knew these types of questions would be taxing to the retail store owners and would shift the focus of the interview away from understanding how a participant viewed his or her world and to conversation-stopping, yes-or-no answers. In exploring the issues with the client, we discovered that the client had a team of vendor representatives who regularly serviced each of the retail outlets. These representatives could easily fill out a physical survey of each store as part of their regular visits. By moving data gathering for this type of information from interviews with a limited number of store owners to a physical survey done by the reps, the client got a national picture of store layout and display in a more cost-efficient manner (no cost for data gathering). This allowed us to devote more interview time to subjects that would generate insights into the way our participants made sense of their businesses.

If you're required to ask questions that just don't seem to fit, we recommend incorporating them at the end of the data gathering, especially if the questions are likely to fatigue the participant. For example, in one study, we were asked to incorporate a two-page rating scale evaluating various business attributes. This amounted to reading two pages of survey questions one by one to participants and having them answer "very important," "somewhat important," "neither," "somewhat unimportant," or "very unimportant." Then the participants were asked to rank order the attributes. By the end of the list, they didn't stand a chance of remembering what they were to rank. Aside from the questions being taxing, the numbers generated were not externally valid due to the limited number of respondents in the study. By putting these questions at the end, we were able to get the information we needed for good strategy upfront before tiring the participants or irritating them with a tedious task that might cause them to walk away from the interview. When reporting inappropriately derived data, be sure to note the limitations of interpretation.

SUMMARY

Balancing research ideals with real-world constraints can be difficult, but with creativity and experience, you can usually get the information you need. Throughout the book and especially in this chapter, we've shared examples and suggestions for overcoming resource problems when executing qualitative research. Whether it be finding panel participants through the Parent Teacher Association at your child's school or arguing for the resources and/or questions you need to generate the type of data that will fuel good strategy, the one thing to keep in mind is your ultimate research goal. As we've stated several times, that goal is to understand how your targeted consumers make sense of their world. Keeping the goal in mind will help you navigate the barriers of time, budget, differences of opinion among the strategy team, and so on, and ultimately will lead you to good consumer insights on which to base your advertising.

KEY TERMS

agency-wide research initiatives: Research initiatives that allow the agency to pool knowledge and resources to serve groups of clients who may share common target markets or a common product category.

context: Where the phenomenon happens. Sometimes, the context can be commonplace, such as working from home. Other times, context may be a mind-set (e.g., environmental activism).

hard numbers: A term frequently, and mistakenly, used to imply that quantitative data are always superior to other types of data.

interviewer-administered survey: A traditional quantitative survey implemented by the researcher, who reads the questions and response options to a participant and then records the participant's answers. This type of survey does not match our definition of qualitative research.

investment: An outlay of capital with the expectation of a return. We feel well-designed research is an investment rather than an expenditure.

mandatory questions: Questions that a client requires be asked during a research project.

partner: A codeveloper of strategy. We feel that researchers and planners are partners in the strategy development process, rather than one serving as a supplier to the other. This means that planners and researchers should have an ongoing two-way dialogue about the marketer's situation, the types of data needed, and the types of insights the research is revealing.

redundancy criterion: When thematic redundancy emerges from the research analysis; the signal that you've recruited enough research participants.

reflection: Taking the time to think about what you've heard during the research process rather than rushing to produce instant feedback for your client or agency.

EXERCISES

1. Take a look at your agency's client roster. If you're a student, go to the *Standard Directory of Advertising Agencies*, pick an agency, and examine its client roster. Based on the roster, where can the agency develop research initiatives that could serve multiple clients? What types of research should be done?

2. You are working for a national marketer of prepared foods. This marketer has identified "soccer moms" as a prime target market. Your job is to find out what it is like to be a soccer mom and how these women make decisions about foods to serve at home. Do you need to field a national research project? How would you defend your answer? What is the context for this phenomenon? What kind of study would you do if you had a research budget of $25,000? How could you generate the same quality of insights with a research budget of $5,000?

RELATED READING

Johnson, J. L., & Laczniak, R. N. (1990). Antecedents of dissatisfaction in advertiser-agency relationships: A model of decision making and communication patterns. *Current Issues and Research in Advertising*, *13*(1), 45–59.

Mitchell, P., & Sanders, N. (1995). Loyalty in agency-client relations: The impact of the organizational context. *Journal of Advertising Research*, *35*(2), 9–22.

9

Evaluating the Work of Planners and Parting Thoughts

By this point, it's probably pretty clear that the qualitative methods used by planners and the way they sometimes go about the process of finding out things can differ substantially from what you usually encounter in communication research. And along with innovative research, other benefits of engaging in planning—better teamwork; a keen understanding of purchase decisions, how consumers relate to brands, and how advertising works in specific circumstances; helping win new business by instilling confidence in prospective clients; stimulating more productive contact between the creative department and the consumer; and so on—can be intangible and difficult to measure. On the surface, evaluating the outcomes of planning seems challenging.

But evaluate we must, as clients have a huge interest in how their money is spent and whether that spending is balanced with a sufficient return on investment (ROI). ROI is the gauge of your communication efforts' effectiveness (i.e., how much you made relative to how much you invested). Calculating ROI for advertising and account planning has been somewhat problematic. For instance, it's sometimes hard to isolate the exact effect of a message, let alone the effect of interviews, ethnographies, and so on that went into developing that message. So if attaching a dollar figure to planning is difficult, how exactly do we evaluate a planner's efforts? This chapter is designed to give you some insight into that question. Additionally, we leave you with some parting thoughts on using qualitative research in your career.

HOW IT IS AND HOW IT SHOULD BE

A couple years back, there were several popular press books on planning, none of which covered the topic of evaluation. That led us to conduct a few studies that examined this and other aspects of planning. Specifically, one of the things we looked at was how the work of planners *is* evaluated and how planners think their work *should be* evaluated. We also analyzed some award-winning account planning cases in an effort to see what evaluative means were used in exemplary applications of planning (Haley, Morrison, & Taylor, 2007; Morrison & Haley, 2003). The outcomes of these studies gave us a pretty good handle on planning evaluation.

In a national survey of planners, we identified three types of evaluation used to assess planning: standard campaign measures, feedback, and awards and press. Conceptually, these three types are grouped into two general stages of evaluation: (1) evaluation of the process (i.e., feedback during the process) and (2) evaluation of outcomes (i.e., traditional campaign measures and attention from media, ad industry, and other planners via awards or press coverage). What that suggests to us is that planning assessment is ongoing and not limited to single points in a campaign.

Standard campaign measures—the most often used ways to evaluate the work of planners—include measures such as awareness, recall, attitude, purchase intent, achievement of marketing objectives, and increased sales or market share. These also are the most common ways to measure the effectiveness of communication campaigns in general. Also interesting to us was the fact that planners thought these measures were the appropriate ways to measure their work. It's worth noting that the focus on performance as a way to evaluate a planner's job might also be a reflection of the pressures of ROI, in that clients want some measure of accountability at every stage of the campaign process.

While standard campaign measures were the most often used ways to evaluate planning, planners rated "feedback" as the most important. Specifically, this meant feedback from the account and creative teams, as well as from the client. This also makes a lot of sense given that planners interact with all these groups on a daily basis. In fact, our findings indicated that planners desired even more feedback than they received.

The last means of evaluation, awards and press, included awards won for a campaign's creative, awards given specifically for planning, and media coverage (think in terms of all the press commercials that air during the Super Bowl receive). While our planners said that awards, in general, weren't particularly important or useful indicators of their performance, they did think that planning awards should be given more weight than they currently are in evaluating their performance.

EVALUATION MEASURES USED IN AWARD-WINNING PLANNING

The idea of planning awards as a measure of feedback intrigued us. Industry awards serve many purposes, one of which is to identify efforts that the industry considers superlative. So we concluded that looking at award-winning cases from a national competition would give us some insight into planning evaluation. We conducted a qualitative thematic analysis on winning case studies in the *Jay Chiat Planning Awards* books published by the American Association of Advertising Agencies (4A's). These case studies loosely resemble creative briefs but also describe the outcomes of campaigns. They also look at a variety of categories, including services, older brands, and nontraditional campaigns. Conveniently for us, one of the goals of the competition is to demonstrate the business value of planning in terms that clients can identify with (American Association of Advertising Agencies,

2005). Before we turn to evaluation measures, a couple other interesting things we found in our analysis are worth noting:

- The most often mentioned problems planners dealt with were creating awareness and lack of brand differentiation.
- In all but a few cases, planning was used to aid products with existing problems and not for new products.
- The vast majority of research that planners conducted was qualitative. Interviews were the most used method, followed by focus groups and various types of ethnographic activities and projective/elicitation techniques.
- Nontraditional media were most often used for products with young target audiences.

Planning success was primarily illustrated by showing the impact that advertising had on a product or service. Planners used both quantitative and qualitative measures to demonstrate effectiveness, but quantitative measures were the most often mentioned. Financial outcomes such as sales/revenue increases, market share, profitability, ROI, and increases in stock prices/earnings per share were the most commonly reported type of result. Given the heightened emphasis on ROI in today's business world, this makes complete sense.

Quantitative attitudinal measures such as attitude toward the brand and ad recall were also identified as evidence of planning success. Other commonly mentioned quantitative measures included metrics such as direct responses either via telephone, website visits, or other consumer inquiries. We also thought it interesting that some quantitative measures were specific to the goals of the campaign but would have little application for other products. For example, Nielsen ratings were presented as evidence of success for a case involving the launch of a new cable network. In another instance, the amount of donated media time in a pro bono campaign was used as evidence of planning success. This suggested to us that designing an appropriate evaluation plan involves creativity.

In addition to the quantitative measure, qualitative measures also were provided as evidence of planning effectiveness. The most common measure was "buzz." Examples of buzz included a brand becoming "social currency," online chatter about a product, and posters related to a brand's products becoming collector's items. Press coverage of a campaign was specifically cited in several cases as contributing to buzz. Buzz took the form of product placements in media (e.g., *Sex and the City* actresses wearing certain rings) and character appearances (e.g., a product's spokesperson appearing on TV talk shows). In one instance, an account planner's promotion was given as evidence of planning effectiveness.

The analysis of the cases and our survey of planners proved immensely helpful in understanding how the work of planners is valued and in identifying things to be concerned about regarding evaluation. One of the goals of the 4A's planning awards is to demonstrate the business value of planning in terms the clients can identify with. This could account for the predominance of quantitative financial results reported in the cases. Clients understand sales, market share, profits, and so on, so it's not surprising that these measures were prominently discussed in the winning cases. However, relying heavily on quantitative measures that evaluate an entire campaign to assess the effects of account planning underscores a long-standing problem with measurements of advertising effectiveness. It's often impossible to separate the distinctive contribution of advertising from the contribution of the overall marketing efforts. Likewise, it's impossible to separate the contribution of planning from the overall communication effort. The moral of the story is to think seriously about what you are trying to accomplish and come up with a way to articulate whether you were successful or not. Because in an age of ROI, if you don't have measures specific to account planning, the planning process may suffer when budgets are tight.

PARTING THOUGHTS

We hope that after reading this book, you have a more solid grounding in qualitative research for the development of advertising and marketing campaigns. Having a solid grounding means understanding the theoretical underpinnings and overall goals of qualitative research. It also means having knowledge of the variety of qualitative research methods available to you and the ability to evaluate those methods so you can select the best one for your particular research problem. Finally, a solid grounding means that you understand how to listen to your consumers and how to communicate what you learn to the rest of the creative team.

Being a qualitative researcher is not just an approach to business; it's a way of viewing the world. Qualitative researchers have a centrality about them. Their lives and their jobs represent similar ways of viewing the world. It's easy to say that qualitative researchers are always on the job, because their natural curiosity about things doesn't turn on or shut off at certain hours of the day. Going to the movies, a rock concert, or a county fair provides the opportunity to observe how people behave. Standing in line at an ATM or supermarket checkout is a prime opportunity to figure out the silent rules governing waiting social behavior. What is the appropriate distance to stand behind a person making a cash withdrawal from an ATM? Is the personal space demanded greater or less than that required in the supermarket line? Obviously, these are things that every shopper must determine implicitly. For the qualitative researcher, heightened self-awareness allows her not only to fit in the line but also to identify the rules others follow. For those involved in advertising, this translates into a belief that no advertising can be effective unless consumers are understood; understanding consumers is imperative to understanding meaning, and that understanding of meaning is subsequently used as the basis for strategy development.

As we've shown you, effective qualitative research begins with developing good basic interviewing skills. Whether you are engaging in participant observation, conducting Internet-based research, or using projective techniques, the core skill is interviewing— knowing what types of questions to ask, how to ask them, and how to listen to your consumers. In addition, knowing when and how to ask follow-up questions will enhance your interviewing skills and allow you to probe into important issues that may lead you to key consumer insights.

Much talk in planning revolves around innovation. Agencies are often looking for the latest techniques to help the strategic team think outside the box. The search for innovative tools also is used as a way to give agencies a competitive advantage in new business pitches. However, we see innovation in research in a somewhat different light. We believe innovation comes when you match the appropriate qualitative method with your information needs in a way that allows the strategy team to gain an emic understanding of how your consumers understand their world. This emic understanding feeds the creative process so innovative strategies can be developed to break through the commercial clutter, resonate with your consumers, and lead to the fulfillment of your client's business objectives.

But innovation doesn't end with simply being research savvy. We've tried to convey that it also means being alert and aware of your research surroundings so you can make connections between seemingly unconnected things. These are the types of connections that help you uncover consumer insights that lead to great advertising. The process of finding these insights makes the job of an advertising researcher unique.

Research is an essential part of strategy development. As such, it requires teamwork—that team being the planner, the researcher, the creatives, account management, the client, and your targeted consumers. Research should not be separated from the planning or strategy development process. Instead of talking about research suppliers, we suggest talking about research partners. Quality research integrated at all stages of the planning process enhances teamwork by actively bringing the consumer to the strategy table. Furthermore, we're confident that good qualitative research is the best way to bring your consumer to that table.

THOUGHTS ON BUILDING YOUR TOOLBOX

The best advertising researchers have a variety of tools in their research toolbox to help them make the best decisions for their clients. We hope this book adds some key tools to your toolbox. And though this book has focused on qualitative research, you might also want to stock your toolbox with good market data and consumer trends, lists of experts for specific product areas in which you work, critical thinking skills, a healthy curiosity about human nature, and your own personal experiences. Oh, and don't forget to throw in some books on human behavior (visit the psychology, sociology, and anthropology sections of your local bookstore); it's always nice to have a couple "how-to" manuals to refer to when you're dealing with humans! When you fill your toolbox with these things, creating advertising will be infinitely easier.

Don't let your toolbox sit in the basement gathering dust. As we've mentioned in several places in this book, the tools we've told you about may seem foreign at first; they will become second nature to you only if you use them. We encourage you to experiment with the techniques you've learned in this book and to add a few other tools to your arsenal to discover what works best for you. We wish you well in this adventure.

Appendix 1

Conducting a Long Interview

This appendix consists of three parts: (1) an assignment; (2) a sample, annotated interview transcript; and (3) a sample write-up of one summary statement from a set of interviews. Good luck conducting your first long interview. No interview is perfect, and everyone gets better with practice!

ASSIGNMENT

1. The objective of your research is, first of all, to understand what, how, and why a sample of men 55+ buy things and, secondly, how, if at all, they use "senior discounts." So the first order of the day is to find an employed male 55+ who is willing to spend some time with you. Do not interview someone you know well, such as a relative or a close neighbor. You may have to "ask around" until you find someone who meets the requirement, perhaps a coworker of a friend or colleague.

Begin your in-depth interview with "Tell me about yourself." Follow that with "Tell me about some things you have bought recently." For each item mentioned, probe with questions such as, How did you happen to buy that particular one? Where did you buy it? Why did you buy it? Summarize as appropriate during the interview.

2. Hopefully, during the general portion of the interview, your research participant will have mentioned or alluded to "senior prices," "senior discounts," "senior rates," or other special pricing available to persons age 55+. If so, when something such as "I got a senior coffee at Krystal's" is mentioned, then you want to probe with questions such as these:

a. Tell me more about special prices for men 55+.

b. Do you look for special prices for customers age 55+?

c. Have you bought other items that were specially priced for men age 55+?

d. How do you feel about such pricing strategies?

e. What do you think about such strategies?

If your participant has not mentioned the issue of special pricing, then you must gently introduce it with "interview extenders" such as these:

a. Some companies, such as restaurants and department stores, have special pricing just for men and women 55+. Have you ever noticed that? Have you ever bought something at a special price just for customers 55+?

b. Has a clerk ever asked you if you wanted a senior discount? If so, how did you feel about that? Did you take it?

SAMPLE INTERVIEW

Below is a transcript from a researcher's first long interview. How well did the researcher accomplish the objectives set out in the assignment? Comments have been inserted into the transcription to help you "think your way" through the interview process.

I: Thank you for agreeing to talk with me. Just so you know, you don't have to answer any questions you don't want to.

P: OK.

I: Is it OK for me to record the interview?

P: Sure.

I: Great! Let's get started. First, tell me a little about yourself.

P: I'm 63 years old, got married about a year ago. I am a grandfather and have three grandchildren who live with me in the manager's apartment at the motel where I work. I'm from North Carolina and moved here 37 years ago to go to school after serving in the army and never left.

{You may be curious how, at 63 years of age, the participant is recently married and a grandfather of three. Resist the urge to satisfy your curiosity when it does not advance the purpose of the interview. If it is important and related, it will be revealed at a later point.}

I: Good. I'm studying what people buy, so could you tell me about some things you bought recently?

P: How recently?

I: Whatever "recent" is to you. It doesn't matter. Just things that you've bought.

{Try not to put unnecessary restraints on the definition of terms.}

P: Well, last week, I bought my grandson his first four-wheeler. It's a little red one, and we have been riding it around the complex here during work to get to rooms quicker. It's actually funny. I see myself using it more than he does until the summer.

{Resist the urge to ask who the four-wheeler is really for, but do note the strong connection between how the participant introduces himself (as a grandfather) and the first purchase he talks about (for one of his grandsons).}

I: Anything else?

{This question could just as easily have been, "Anything else for your grandson?"}

P: Well, today I went to the grocery store to get some things for dinner tonight and get a pack of cigarettes. Then I bought some work tools and some new work shirts and pants on Wednesday.

{The interviewer needs to remember to ask about (1) things for dinner, (2) work tools, and (3) work shirts and pants. We do not learn much about the purchase of the tools and the work clothes.}

I: Tell me about buying things for dinner.

P: I buy food on a regular basis for the family. I go to the grocery store at least three times a week since it is so close to us. Then I buy gas on a weekly basis at the station up the street. I get my car washed every Sunday, weather permitting, at the car wash across the street because they do car washes for half price on Sunday. I buy a pack of cigarettes every day.

I: Tell me how you decided to buy the four-wheeler.

{It would be better to follow up on work tools and work clothes and then circle back to the four-wheeler.}

P: I looked around for good deals at different places, and I waited for the right price until I found it on sale. I found it for 20% off. With the other things I have bought recently, I went to Walmart to get my work clothes and Home Depot to buy my work tools because they carry everything I will ever need in my job. I always go to Kroger to get all of the groceries I get throughout the week because it is right down the street. Then I generally get gas at whatever gas station has the cheapest gas around.

I: When you were talking about looking around at the prices for the four-wheeler, what was it that you were looking for?

P: Obviously, the price. I looked into different prices for different brands, and then I looked into what I could afford. When I figured out what four-wheeler I wanted, it just boiled down to waiting and looking around for someone to sell me the four-wheeler at that price.

I: Is that what led you to buy the four-wheeler at the place you did?

P: Well, they were actually having a clearance sale on the four-wheeler. I got it for 20% off, which made it cheaper than I was even willing to spend on it.

I: Do you look for discounts on anything else?

P: I do look through the Sunday paper coupon section, and I also get senior citizen discounts at certain places where I shop.

{The participant leads us to what we want to discuss, and along the way, he has indicated that he is price conscious in his buying. Note that we did not ask, "Do you use senior discounts?" and we now have a context for understanding why this participant does.}

I: Tell me more about senior citizen discounts.

P: I'm so old that most of the stores I shop at are nice enough to give me discounts on things I buy!

{No false flattery such as, "You don't look that old!"}

I: What are some of these places?

P: Mainly, I just use the discounts for the groceries, and that's just certain days. I shop at Walmart because they are really cheap and I can get discounts on some things there, and I take advantage when I take my grandchildren or wife to the movies whenever we go. I can save generally at least 2 dollars at the movies nowadays, and that's a lot with the price of a movie ticket now. I remember back when a movie barely cost anything.

{Resist the urge to move the discussion to the "good old days."}

I: Do you typically look for deals and discounts?

P: Oh, yes.

I: Where?

P: At restaurants and things like that.

I: Any particular ones?

P: Yeah, Colonel Sanders! (laughs)

I: You go there often?

P: Yeah, we like to go there on Sundays. There and Captain D's.

I: Do you go anywhere just because of the discount?

P: Shoney's, McDonald's, Burger King, Hardee's, places like that. We'll look for coupons in the paper, stuff like that.

{Interviewer should ask about places other than fast-food restaurants.}

I: Do you ever ask people if they offer a discount?

P: No. At most places, when I get the discount, I'll see it somewhere in their store about the senior discount or someone will actually ask me if I qualify for the discount because I look so old. Which is nice of them, I guess. Risky but nice.

I: Why do you say that?

P: I mean, it isn't always appropriate to just randomly ask someone his age. Some people would get offended, I'm sure, if asked their age. For all they know, I could be a lot younger than I look, which would be nice. It's risky for them because you never want to offend the customers that they are trying to serve.

I: How do you feel about these special discounts for seniors?

P: I think it is a great idea businesswise. I know that senior citizens are stereotyped as being cheap or stingy when it comes to buying things. I would have to say they're right, too, when I think about the buying habits of some of my friends. Some of my friends will only shop at certain stores that offer senior discounts.

I: Can you give me an example?

P: I know a guy who never misses a senior discount day for groceries. He always reminds me on that day that the discount is going on. He almost always goes and buys an excessive amount of dog food, meat, and charcoal. He stocks up on all of these things until the next time that the senior discount is available. It's funny to me.

I: What do you mean by "funny"?

P: I just don't shop that way. I buy things when I need them. I don't like having a bunch of things cluttering up my apartment.

I: You've mentioned using senior discounts at the movies, when buying groceries, and at fast-food restaurants. Can you think of any other places where you've gotten a senior discount?

{Pausing and summarizing helps both parties collect their thoughts and sometimes triggers additional recall.}

P: I know some men who get a discount at the golf course. I don't play golf, so I never have myself.

I: Anything else come to mind?

{Always give the participant plenty of time to think of other things; don't feel as though you have to close the interview at some appointed time.}

P: About senior discounts?

I: Yes.

P: No, nothing else.

I: Well, thank you so very much for talking to me. You've really helped me out.

P: Glad to do it.

SAMPLE PAGE FROM A QUALITATIVE REPORT

Coding an interview involves breaking down the transcripts into meaningful units and then reassembling the data in an understandable form. One of the more accessible ways to do this is through the writing of summary statements, which are then supported by examples from the transcripts. A one-page example follows. Note that qualitative reports deal with the essence of things, not with enumerating them. Because sample size is typically small, using exact counts or percentages, which suggest patterns of distributions, are avoided. Let your participants' words provide the examples.

Summary Statement: The presence and actions of others influence the perception and use of senior citizen discounts. This includes the actions of retail clerks, friends, and family.

Some men depend on retail personnel to recognize that they are eligible for a discount and to give it to them automatically. Participant 2 noted,

Sometimes, I think at certain restaurants they just give it to me. I think it's pretty obvious . . . that I would get the senior discount if they asked my age.

Some men are influenced by referral or suggestion from others. Noting the influence of friends, Participant 6 said,

> They'll pass it along and say, "Hey, you need to talk to so-and-so at this particular business because they can give you a discount."

Participant 8 noted the influence of his spouse:

> She always makes sure to take me to Belk (for clothes) on their Senior Day.

In addition to the actions of retail clerks, the suggestions of friends, and the influence of family members, going shopping or attending events with others seems to increase the use of senior discounts. Participant 6 noted,

> If a group of us are together and they are all taking advantage of it (senior discount), then, sure, I will use it.

And Participant 8 revealed,

> Sometimes, I go see movies with a group of men that I know, and, believe me, they all take advantage of the senior rate.

Thus, whether men use a senior citizen discount is often determined by the presence or absence of others. The presence of others—especially other seniors—seems to have a positive effect. However, the behavior of retail clerks or the mere presence of unknown others may have a negative effect, as revealed in these interactions.

Appendix 2

Putting Your Skills to Use

1. Kenneth Cole Watches

Among older teens and young adults, watch wearing is on the decline. The wristwatch has been replaced with smartphones or other personal electronic devices. However, the watch industry isn't ready to give up. They know that if they can get people accustomed to wearing watches in their younger adult years, those people will likely be lifelong watch wearers.

Kenneth Cole, a fashion marketer with a strong young adult following, makes a line of affordable and fashionable watches. Kenneth Cole watches have the style and price point to make them a perfect watch option for college students and young professionals. However, these college students and young professionals aren't wearing watches.

Your marketing challenge is to reinvigorate watch sales among this age group by motivating them to buy and wear Kenneth Cole watches. Where do you start? You guessed it. You start with good qualitative research.

- What are the objectives of your research?
- Who do you need to research?
- What do you need to find out from them?
- How are you going to do it?

2. Fortified Drinking Water for Dogs

America is a pet-crazy nation. In fact, the United States has the highest percentage of households with dogs and cats. We love our animals, and 9 out of 10 owners consider their pets to be members of the family. We buy them birthday and holiday gifts, we sign their names on greeting cards, and we prominently display their pictures in our homes and wallets. We also consider them when we make large purchases, such as cars ("Will Fido fit in the back seat?").

In short, pets are big business, with Americans spending more than $10 billion annually on pet supplies and over-the-counter medicines (Bennett, 2010). It's no wonder, then, that the industry has caught the attention of one of the world's largest beverage companies. This company wants to enter the pet industry with a fortified drinking water for dogs. The product will be packaged similarly to bottled water for humans and will be priced in the same range.

Despite months of research and a large investment in product development, the company is still undecided whether to continue with its efforts. Lots of statistics on the pet industry suggest that the product would be successful, but what's lacking is a real understanding of the meaning of dogs to the people who own them. That's where the company needs your help as a qualitative researcher.

- Design and execute a research project aimed at determining the meaning of dogs to the people who own them.
- Are there segments of dog owners who would be more likely to purchase this product? What are their characteristics?
- What should the product be called?
- What creative strategy do you recommend to introduce this product to the market?
- How can this creative strategy be parlayed into advertising, public relations, and sales promotion strategies?

3. McCormick & Company

The economy seems to be on everyone's minds lately. High unemployment, the credit crunch, uncertainty about the future—all these factors influence a variety of consumer segments and product sales. The food industry is not immune to these changes; rising food costs and cultural trends affect consumer shopping and eating behaviors. One result is that people are cooking at home more regularly; however, this is truer of people over the age of 35 than it is of young adults. This trend obviously has implications for the spice/seasoning industry and the largest company in this category, McCormick & Company.

McCormick needs to identify new consumer segments to sustain and grow the company. McCormick has decided that post-college young adults (those who have their first career job, just got married, are anticipating children, or are new parents, etc.) offer the most promise for obtaining this goal. McCormick's reasoning is simple: If it can establish a relationship with younger cooks, then they will become brand-loyal and lifelong users of McCormick spices. There's just one problem: These are the adults who are least likely to cook.

Your task is to convince young adults to begin cooking/cook more and, more importantly, to use McCormick spices. Using qualitative research, develop a research agenda that will allow you to get to know how these folks live their lives.

- Psychographically, what are they like?
- How much time do they have for cooking?
- In their view, what are the pros and cons of cooking?
- What foods do they tend to eat?
- What's the difference between a meal prepared at home and fast food/takeout?
- What appeals would be most effective in influencing them to cook more?

Appendix 3

Disney's Animal Kingdom Theme Park: A Case Study

Walt Disney World is the No. 1 tourist attraction in the United States. It's an ever-expanding offering of theme parks, resorts, shopping, recreation, dining, and fun in Central Florida. Its most recent theme park addition is Disney's Animal Kingdom Park (DAK).

DAK, though more than 10 years old now, faces a problem. People still don't really know what it is. Is it a zoo? After all, it features live animal attractions. But it also features thrill rides, Broadway-style shows, cultural and educational attractions, interesting dining experiences, shopping, and more.

Initial research showed that people thought of DAK as "Disney does a zoo." This thought wasn't as motivating to families as messages developed for other Disney parks. Yet DAK has grown in popularity and offerings. It is the largest of the four Walt Disney World theme parks—in fact, the entire Magic Kingdom Park could sit within the acreage devoted to one of DAK's major attractions.

THE MARKETING CHALLENGE

Here's the marketing challenge: Motivate the primary family vacation decision maker to add DAK to the family's Walt Disney World vacation. That is, we don't want them to visit DAK instead of another Disney park; rather, we want them to extend their stay and spend at least a day at DAK.

Your first step: Because the consumer image of DAK is unclear, you must define the park's "brand essence." That is, what is the brand promise for the park? What is the core idea that drives the park? What holds its diverse offerings together conceptually?

How are you going to figure this out? What is an appropriate research plan?

Here's how students using this case as an advertising campaigns class assignment approached the problem and what they learned using qualitative research within an account planning paradigm.

Finding the Brand Essence

First, the students watched a film produced by Disney about the making of DAK. From this, they learned that the three key design principles of the park were "entertainment, adventure, and conservation awareness."

Sometimes, what designers intend doesn't actually come through in the final execution, so the students needed to experience the park for themselves. They hopped in vans and went on a work trip to Disney World!

Site Visit Research

Instead of just visiting the park, the students engaged in various research experiences while there. This research was not officially sanctioned by Disney, so the students were very, very careful not to bother guests or pretend to be representatives of Disney. Instead, the students wanted to understand the experience of the park firsthand.

Diaries

Each student carried a small notebook and pen throughout the day. In it, they recorded their personal observations about the park. The diaries went beyond just an itinerary of what they did that day; students were asked to record their reactions to the park and the feelings they experienced when seeing the various areas and attractions. They were asked to note the colors used in the park, the music, the architecture, the storytelling elements, landscaping, words used in park scripts, and so on.

Photo Essay

In addition to written diaries, students were asked to make a photo essay of what they felt was the "essence" of the park. At first, the photos were of the park attributes (e.g., rides, attractions, shows, buildings, foliage). But as the day progressed, students noticed that the essence of the park wasn't in the attractions themselves but, rather, in how people interacted with those attractions and one another while there. The subject of the photographs shifted from attractions to people.

Interviews

Students also talked with people during the day as they stood in lines or rested on park benches, and so on. As most of the students were first-time DAK visitors, it was quite natural for them to ask other park guests for recommendations on what to do, what they liked about the park, and so on. The students found the park guests eager to instruct and guide first-time visitors as to the ins and outs of the DAK experience.

Students were required to experience every attraction, show, shop, and trail, and at least two restaurants during their visit.

Post-Visit Research

Afterward, exhausted, students had to write a diary summary capturing their overall reflections of the day and what the park meant to them.

Back home, students were asked to find and interview DAK park enthusiasts (i.e., those people who love DAK). Some interviews were conducted face to face; others were facilitated through interactive technology, depending on where the participant was located. In these interviews, enthusiasts were asked questions such as, "What makes Disney's Animal Kingdom Park special?" and "What would you tell others about Disney's Animal Kingdom Park?"

The Brand Essence

So what did the students find was the brand essence of DAK? The students determined that DAK is a "Celebration of Life."

The park is an active experience. It's positive in tone. It's about conservation challenges and successes. It's all about the relationship between humans and the natural world. Every aspect of DAK celebrates life in a fun, adventurous, and educational way.

How to Make DAK Relevant to the Primary Family Vacation Decision Maker in the Household

The next step was to research who the primary family vacation decision maker is and what she or he wants and needs. Doing this required more interviews.

Students started to recruit parents of school-aged children (based on secondary data regarding Disney theme park visitors). Long individual interviews were conducted with one or two parents, depending on who was available and the preference of the participants. In these interviews, the parents were asked to describe their ideal family vacation. They were asked to relay positive and negative family vacation experiences. They were also asked to talk about their aspirations for their kids.

The Findings

What do parents want from a family vacation?

- Quality time with the kids. Why? Daily life is over-scheduled and stressful. They don't have enough time to get to know their kids.

- Must satisfy extended family. Why? Families are traveling with aunts, uncles, grandparents, and other family members. This puts stress on the vacation decision maker to find a destination that will satisfy diverse interests and needs of the family.
- They want a vacation they can feel good about. Why? Parents want enriching experiences for their kids that are fun.
- Parents want to be heroes in their kids' eyes. Why? Who wouldn't?
- Parents want to be able to brag to other parents about the great vacation they had. Why? They want to be seen as good parents by their peers.

Next Step: What Does DAK Offer That Matches What These Parents Want?

The good news is that DAK meets these parents' needs to a T! DAK offers activities that are appealing to Grandma and the kids. DAK is a park with a purpose; that is, it's a fun, enriching experience that parents can feel good about. DAK offers quality interactive experiences in which parents and kids can participate together.

Now, how to turn the insights into creative strategy?

Creative Strategy Research

Based on all the original research, students started to brainstorm creative strategy options that would convey the brand essence of DAK in a way that would motivate parents to take their families to the park. They narrowed the ideas to five and held focus group interviews with target market parents to discuss the options.

Based on the discussion, the students determined that the creative strategy relevant for the target market was, "Disney's Animal Kingdom is a sensory experience in which families discover new life from around the world." Now, the actual creative strategy statement rarely appears in any execution, but the statement focuses the creative team on what needs to be communicated. Parents responded well to the family discovery and rejuvenation and active sensory experience aspects of the strategy. They felt this was different from other theme park advertising messages and thought it would make them curious about DAK.

The research revealed insights that drove advertising execution decision specifically:

- From the interviews, the students learned that the ads had to be visual and let parents see inside the park, since knowledge level about the park was relatively low.
- The ads would have to show traditional Disney elements and communicate what is unique about DAK.
- The ads would have to stress family interaction, fun, and learning—in that order.

Based on these insights, the students developed a highly visual, sensory campaign using exploration metaphors, rhythmic copy, and bright natural-element colors, with the tag "Come to Life— Disney's Animal Kingdom Park."

Qualitative research also was used to refine the creative executions. Each execution was shown to target market members, and they were asked what the ad said to them. They were asked if the ad would make them interested in visiting DAK and if it would get their attention. These semistructured, open-ended interviews also gave the participants a chance to say whatever they wanted to say about the ads.

References

American Association of Advertising Agencies. (2005). *Jay Chiat Awards for account planning*. New York, NY: Author.

American Association of Advertising Agencies. (2008). *Awards for account planning 2007*. New York, NY: Author.

Atkin, D. (1997, July 21). Planning for the present. *Adweek, 38*(29), 34.

Barry, T. E., Peterson, R. L., & Todd, W. B. (1987). The role of account planning in the future of advertising agency research. *Journal of Advertising Research, 27*(1).

Bengston, R. E. (1982). A powerful qualitative marketing research tool, one-on-one depth interviewing has 7 advantages. *Marketing News, 15*(23), 21.

Bennett, L. (2010, January 14). *Pet industry trends for 2010*. Retrieved March 1, 2011, from http://smallbiztrends.com/2010/01/pet-industry-trends-for-2010.html

Berg, B. L. (1989). *Qualitative research methods for the social sciences*. Needham Heights, MA: Allyn & Bacon.

Boddy, C. (2005). Projective techniques in market research: Valueless subjectivity or insightful reality? *International Journal of Market Research, 47*(3), 239–254.

Boyko, R. (1999, July). *The evolution of an idea*. Paper presented at the Account Planning Conference, San Diego, CA.

Bragen, H. (2000). In online focus groups, it's the way they write. *Marketing News, 34*(8), 8.

British Account Planning Group. (n.d.). *What is an account planner?* Retrieved August 13, 2001, from www.onlymarketing.com/htm/p05.htm

Campbell Mithun Esty: MoneyGram. (1999, July 12). *Adweek, 40*(28), 6a.

Capon, N., & Scammon, D. (1979). Advertising agency decisions: An analytic treatment. *Current Issues and Research in Advertising, 2*(1), 35–52.

Collins, C. (2000, July 6). Focus groups go online to measure the appeal of websites. *New York Times, 149*(51441), 8.

Commercial Market Strategies. (2001, August 6). *Jordan uses projective techniques to guide communication campaign*. Retrieved August 6, 2001, from http://cmsproject.com/news/articles/jordan_projective.cfm?view=normal

Denzin, N. K., & Lincoln, Y. S. (1994). Introduction: Entering the field of qualitative research. In N. K. Denzin & Y. S. Lincoln (Eds.), *Handbook of qualitative research* (pp. 1–17). Thousand Oaks, CA: Sage.

Donoghue, S. (2000). Projective techniques in consumer research. *Journal of Family Ecology and Consumer Sciences, 28,* 47–53.

Felton, G. (1994). *Advertising: Concept and copy.* Englewood Cliffs, NJ: Prentice Hall.

Fortini-Campbell, L. (1992). *Hitting the sweet spot.* Chicago, IL: Copy Workshop.

Fortini-Campbell, L. (2001). *Hitting the sweet spot* (2nd ed.). Chicago, IL: Copy Workshop.

Fram, E. H., & Cibotti, E. (1991). The shopping list studies and projective techniques. *Marketing Research, 3*(1), 14–20.

Furgurson, J. (2000). *The agency creative brief.* Retrieved August 13, 2001, from www.adwords.com/ad_side/ad_brief.htm

Ganesh, J., & Oakenfull, G. (1999). International product positioning: An illustration using perceptual mapping techniques. *Journal of Global Marketing, 13*(2), 85–111.

Glaser, B., & Strauss, A. (1967). *The discovery of grounded theory.* Chicago, IL: Aldine.

Goldring, J. (1997). Netting the cybershark: Consumer protection, cyberspace, the nation-state, and democracy. In B. Kahin & C. Nesson (Eds.), *Borders in cyberspace: Information policy and the global information infrastructure* (pp. 322–354). Cambridge, MA: MIT Press.

Got milk? California Fluid Milk Processors Advisory Board. (1996, August 5). *Adweek, 37*(32), 6.

Greenbaum, T. (2000). Focus groups vs. online. *Advertising Age, 71*(7), 34.

GroupM forecasts global ad spending to surpass $500 billion in 2011. (2010, December 6). Retrieved March 1, 2011, from http://www.groupm.com/bulleting/press-release/groupm-forecasts-global-ad-spending-surpass-500-billion-2011

Haley, E., Morrison, M., & Taylor, R. E. (2007, August). *Excellent account planning: What award-winning planning cases tell us about planning's utility in advertising.* Paper presented at the Association for Education in Journalism and Mass Communication Conference, Washington, D.C.

Hausman, A. (2010, August 3). How to build perceptual maps. *Hausman Marketing Letter.* Retrieved March 3, 2011, from http://hausmanmarketresearch.org/customer-relationship-management/how-to-build-perceptual-maps/

Healthy research/creative marriage translates discovery, imaginative interpretation into ads. (1982). *Marketing News, 15*(23), 13.

Hollander, S. L. (1988). Project techniques uncover *real* consumer attitudes. *Marketing News, 22*(1), 34.

JWT Mumbai: De Beers group marketing (wedding program). (2008). In *American Association of Advertising Agencies awards for account planning 2008* (pp. 171–177). New York, NY: American Association of Advertising Agencies.

Kassarjian, H. H. (1974). Projective methods. In R. Ferber (Ed.), *Handbook of marketing research* (pp. 85–100). New York, NY: McGraw-Hill.

Kirkpatrick, M. (2009, January 20). *Word cloud analysis of Obama's inaugural speech compared to Bush, Clinton, Reagan, Lincoln's*. Retrieved February 27, 2011, from http://www.readwriteweb.com/archives/tag_clouds_of_obamas_inaugural_speech_compared_to_bushs.php

Kover, A. J., & Goldberg, S. M. (1995). The games copywriters play: Conflict, quasi-control, a new proposal. *Journal of Advertising Research, 35*(4), 53–61.

Kover, A. J., James, W. L., & Sonner, B. S. (1997). To whom do advertising creatives write? An inferential answer. *Journal of Advertising Research, 37*(1), 41–53.

Krueger, R. A. (1998). *Developing questions for focus groups*. Thousand Oaks, CA: Sage.

LeFevre, H., Lee, J., Averell, M., & Toth, B. (2010). *The planner survey 2010*. Retrieved from http://www.slideshare.net/hklefevre/the-planner-survey-2010

Mad Dogs & Englishmen: Yoo-hoo chocolate drink. (1999, July 12). *Adweek, 40*(28), 12a.

Mann, C., & Stewart, F. (2000). *Internet communication and qualitative research: A handbook for researching online*. Thousand Oaks, CA: Sage.

Maxwell, A., Wanta, W., & Bentley, C. (2000). *The effectiveness of account planners at U.S. advertising agencies*. Paper presented at the annual meeting of the American Academy of Advertising, Newport, RI.

McCracken, G. (1988). *The long interview*. Newbury Park, CA: Sage.

Morrison, M., & Haley, E. (2003). Account planners' views on how their work is and should be evaluated. *Journal of Advertising, 32*(2), 7–16.

Morrison, M., & Haley, E. (2006). The integration of account planning in U.S. advertising agencies. *Journal of Advertising Research, 46*, 124–132.

Nelson, T., & Kent, M. (1999). The power of conversations. *Adweek Eastern Edition, 40*(28), 3a.

NOP Research Group. (2001, August 6). *Your customers' view of you may be very different from your own perception*. Retrieved from www.nop.co.uk

Patwardhan, P., Patwardhan, H., & Vasavada-Oza, F. (2009). Insights on account planning: A view from the Indian ad industry. *Journal of Current Issues and Research in Advertising, 31*(2), 107–119.

PBS. (2000). *Life on the Internet timeline*. Retrieved September 4, 2001, from www.pbs.org/internet/timeline/index.html

Piirto, R. (1990). Measuring minds in the 1990s. *American Demographics, 12*(12), 30–35.

Qualitative Solutions and Research. (1997). *NUD*IST software for qualitative data analysis*. Thousand Oaks, CA: Sage.

Rabin, A. I. (1981). Projective methods: A historical introduction. In A. I. Rubin (Ed.), *Assessment with projective techniques: A concise introduction* (pp. 1–22). New York, NY: Springer.

Ramsey, E., Ibbotson, P., & McCole, P. (2006). Application of projective techniques in an e-business research context. *International Journal of Market Research, 48*(5), 551–573.

Reid, L., King, K. W., & DeLorme, D. (1998). Top-level agency creatives look at advertising creativity then and now. *Journal of Advertising, 27*(2), 1–15.

Robertson, D. H., & Joselyn, R. W. (1974). Projective techniques in research. *Journal of Advertising Research, 14*(5), 27–31.

Roman, K., & Maas, J. (1992). *The new how to advertise.* New York, NY: St. Martin's.

Scott, P. (1999, May). *Inspiring creativity with better briefs and briefings.* Presentation given at the annual U.S. Account Planning Group Conference, San Diego, CA.

Securing attendance to focus groups: A little time and a lot of persuasion. (2000). *PR News, 56*(6), 8.

Semeonoff, B. (1976). *Projective techniques.* New York, NY: John Wiley.

Smith, A. D. (1989). *The ethnic origin of nations.* New York, NY: Blackwell.

Soley, L. (2006). Measuring responses to commercials: A projective-elicitation approach. *Journal of Current Issues and Research in Advertising, 28*(2), 55–64.

Soley, L. (2010). Projective techniques in U.S. marketing and management research. *Qualitative Market Research, 13*(4), 334–353.

Soley, L., & Smith, A. L. (2008). *Projective techniques for social science and business research.* Milwaukee, WI: Southshore.

Steel, J. (1998). *Truth, lies, and advertising: The art of account planning.* New York, NY: John Wiley.

Steiner, P. (1993). On the Internet, nobody knows you're a dog [Cartoon]. *New Yorker, 69*(20), 61.

Stevens, R. E., Wrenn, B., Ruddick, M. E., & Sherwood, P. K. (1997). *The marketing research guide.* New York, NY: Haworth.

Strauss, A., & Corbin, J. (1998). *Basics of qualitative research.* Thousand Oaks, CA: Sage.

Taylor, R. E. (1994). Qualitative research. In M. Singletary (Ed.), *Mass communication research* (pp. 265–279). New York, NY: Longman.

Teas, K. R., & Grapentine, T. H. (2004). Testing market positioning themes: A perceptual mapping approach. *Journal of Marketing Communications, 10,* 267–288.

Underhill, P. (2000). *Why we buy: The science of shopping.* New York, NY: Touchstone.

Vidich, A. J., & Lyman, S. M. (2000). Qualitative methods: Their history in sociology and anthropology. In N. K. Denzin & Y. S. Lincoln (Eds.), *Handbook of qualitative research* (2nd ed., pp. 37–84). Thousand Oaks, CA: Sage.

Weissman, R. (1998). Online or off target. *American Demographics, 20*(11), 20–21.

Wellner, A. S. (2001). Research on a shoestring: How Bissell steamrolled its way to the top of the category. *American Demographics, 23*(4), 38–39.

White, R. (1995). Planning and its relationship with account management. In *What every account executive should know about account planning.* New York, NY: American Association of Advertising Agencies.

Young, S., Persichitte, K. A., & Tharp, D. D. (1998). Electronic mail interviews: Guidelines for conducting research. *International Journal of Educational Telecommunications, 4*(4), 291–300.

Zikmund, W. G. (1984). *Business research methods.* Fort Worth, TX: Dryden.

Index

Accompanied shopping, 46–47
  See also Participant observation
Account planning, 4
  brand/strategy development.
    See Branding
  consumer and, 7
  difference from traditional
    research, 9
  examples of, 12–17
  function of, 7, 17–18
  history of, 4–7
  innovation and, 9–10,
  role of research in, 8–10
  stages of, 10–12
  training and, 3–4
Account Planning Group U.S.
  (APG-US), 6, 12
American Association of Advertising
  Agencies (4A's), 12, 181–183
ARC Research, 119
ARPANET, 117
Association techniques, 94, 95, 97
  See also Projective techniques
Atkin, D., 12

BBDO Worldwide, 97
Bengston, R. E., 92
Bias, 9, 29, 30, 31, 35–36, 38, 60–61, 133
BMP DDB. *See* Boase Massimi Pollitt
Boase Massimi Pollitt, 4
Brand Asset Valuator, 2
Bragen, H., 119
Branding, 1–4, 5, 16–17, 26–27
  brand/strategy development, 10
British Account Planning Group, 158

CERN, 118
Chiat, J., 6
Choice ordering, 94, 104
  See also Projective techniques
Clearasil, 102

Commercial Market Strategies
  (CMS), 111
Completion techniques, 94, 99–101
  See also Projective techniques
Construction techniques, 94, 97–99
  See also Projective techniques
Consumer advocate, 7, 9
Consumer perspective, 3, 6, 59
Corbin, J., 33
Creative brief, 10–11, 143–144, 145
  advisory to the creative team, 145
  assessment of, 156–158
  components, 149–154
  defined, 144
  examples, 151, 153, 154
  key insight and, 148
  language in, 154–156
  presentation of, 158–159
  revising, 147
  role in campaigns, 145–148
Creative researchers. *See* Account
  planning

Data analysis, 30–36, 75, 109
  coding paradigms, 33–35
  interview data, 75–80
  projective and elicitation techniques,
    107–109
  verisimilitude, 35
  See also Qualitative research
De Beers Group, 14–15
Deductive analysis, 28
  See also Qualitative research
Deprivation studies, 57–58
  Got Milk?, 57–58
  See also Ethnography
Dichter, E., 93
Disney's Animal Kingdom Park
  (DAK), 201–206
Donoghue, S., 91, 94, 104, 108
DoubleClick, 136

E-mail, 83–84, 117, 118, 132–135
Emic analysis. *See* Ethnography
Ethics, 49, 55, 138–139
ETHNOGRAPH, 110
Ethnography, 43–61
  emic analysis, 43
  ethics. *See* Ethics
  etic analysis, 43
  terminating research, 30
  traditions, 43
  See Accompanied shopping, Panel
    studies, Participant observa-
    tion, Qualitative research
Etic analysis. *See* Ethnography
Evaluation, 179–183
  awards and press, 180, 181
  buzz, 182
  feedback, 180, 181
  in award-winning cases, 181–182
  standard campaign measures, 180
  ROI, 179, 181, 182, 183
Expressive techniques, 94, 101–104
  See also Projective techniques

Facebook, 18, 120, 126, 127, 128, 129,
    132, 136, 139
Fortini-Campbell, L., 5, 10, 12, 144,
    148, 151

Goldberg, S. M., 7, 147
Goodby, Silverstein & Partners, 57
Grounded theory, 32
  See also Qualitative research

Haire, M., 93
Haley, E., 145
The House Where the Brand
    Lives, 103

Ibbotson, P., 108
Inductive analysis, 28
  See also Qualitative research
Integrated Marketing Communications
    (IMC), 17–18
Internet, 117–119
Interviewing, 60, 65–85
  account planners, 19–20
  characteristics of a qualitative
    interview, 66–68

conducting an interview, 71–74
data sheet, 70
duration, 67-68
ethics. *See* Ethics
interview guide, 68–70
importance of listening, 60–61
mechanics, 70–71
multiple methods, 38
number in a typical study, 38
panel studies, 56
participant observation, 47–48

J. Walter Thompson (JWT), 4
Jay Chiat Planning Awards, 181–182

Kassarjian, H. H., 93, 95, 97, 100
Kenneth Cole Watches, 197
Kover, A. J., 147
Kraft Foods, 129
Krueger, R. A., 92, 99, 101, 109, 111

Leo Burnett agency, 110

Market Research Organization, 111–112
McCole, P., 108
McCormick & Company, 198–199
Mixed methods, 36–38
  See also Qualitative research
MoneyGram, 13–14
Morrison, M., 145
Multiple methods, 36–38
  See also Qualitative research
MySpace, 139

National Science Foundation, 117–119
NUD*IST, 110

Online surveys, 118
Online interviewing, 132–139
  advantages, 107
  disadvantages, 107
  ethics. *See* Ethics
  planning for, 134
  recruitment. *See* Recruitment
Online focus groups, 119–124
  applications, 119
  asynchronous group, 121, 126–132
  benefits, 120, 122, 126
  challenges, 122–123

ethics. *See* Ethics
moderators and, 124–126
planning for, 124–126
recruitment. *See* Recruitment
synchronous groups, 121–122
trolls, 129–130

Panel studies, 56–58
example, 56
ethnography, 43
interviewing, 65
language of, 27–28
methods, 29–30
nature of, 23–24
sensitized concept, 32
validity and interpretation, 35–36
Participant observations, 45–55
accompanied shopping, 46
issues with, 47–55
Perceptual mapping, 104–107
Photosort, 97
Piirto, R., 97
Planning. *See* Account planning
PR News, 136
Procter & Gamble (P&G), 128
Projective techniques, 89–112
advantages and disadvantages,
107–109
analysis, 109–112
defined, 91
history of, 92–94
nature of stimulus in, 91
reliability and validity of, 107–109
types, 94–107

Qualitative research, 2, 8–10,
23–24
analysis of, 30–36
assumptions of, 25–27
defined, 2
language of, 27–28
methods, 29–30

multiple versus mixed methods,
36–38
nature of data, 30
online, 119
traditions, 24
See also Creative briefs, Ethnography, Evaluation, Projective
techniques

Rabin, A. I., 92–94
Ramsey, E., 108
Recruitment, 50–52, 122,
135–136
list brokers, 138
Research
types, 8–10
appropriateness, 8
See also Qualitative research
Richard's Group, 48

Scott, P., 10–11
Skype, 121–122, 132–133, 134–135
Steam N' Clean, 56
Steel, J., 11, 144, 151
Strauss, A., 28

Text cloud. *See* Word cloud
Thematic Apperception Test (TAT),
101–102
Thomasville Furniture, 48
Triangulation, 28, 30, 38
Twitter, 18, 136–137

University of Tennessee, 2–3

Walt Disney World, 201, 202
Word cloud, 98

Y&R (Young and Rubicam), 2
Yoo–hoo, 16–17

Zikmund, W. G., 102

About the Authors

Margaret A. Morrison is professor in the School of Advertising and Public Relations at the University of Tennessee. She received her PhD from the University of Georgia in 1996. She has taught classes in media planning, account planning, qualitative research, and advertising campaigns at Tennessee since 1995. Her work has appeared in various outlets, such as *Journal of Advertising Research, Journal of Advertising, Journal of Current Issues and Research in Advertising,* and *American Journal of Public Health.*

Eric Haley is professor in the School of Advertising and Public Relations at the University of Tennessee. He received his PhD from the University of Georgia in 1992. He teaches a variety of advertising courses and a doctoral seminar in qualitative research. He is an active research consultant, helping national clients with custom research information needs. His publications have appeared in *Journal of Advertising, Journal of Advertising Research, Journal of Consumer Affairs,* and *Journal of Current Issues and Research in Advertising.*

Kim Bartel Sheehan is professor at the University of Oregon's School of Journalism and Communication and directs the Masters Program in Strategic Communication. She received her PhD from the University of Tennessee. Her teaching and research interests include online consumer behavior and research methods, interactivity and social media, small-business marketing, and advertising creative strategy. Her research has appeared in *Journal of Advertising, Journal of Advertising Research,* and *Journal of Public Policy and Marketing,* and she is the author of *Controversies in Contemporary Advertising,* also published by SAGE.

Ronald E. Taylor is professor in the School of Advertising and Public Relations at the University of Tennessee. He earned an AB in journalism at the University of North Carolina at Chapel Hill, and an MS in advertising and a PhD in communications at the University of Illinois at Urbana-Champaign. He has taught courses in qualitative research at Tennessee for the past 25 years.

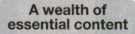
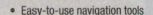